Witch Power

*This book is dedicated to my Aunty Elizabeth:
I love you and I miss you.*

Witch Power
Hexing the Patriarchy with Feminist Magic

EMMA QUILTY

polity

Copyright © Emma Quilty 2026

The right of Emma Quilty to be identified as Author of this Work has been asserted in accordance with the UK Copyright, Designs and Patents Act 1988.

First published in 2025 by Polity Press Ltd.

Polity Press Ltd.
65 Bridge Street
Cambridge CB2 1UR, UK

Polity Press Ltd.
111 River Street
Hoboken, NJ 07030, USA

All rights reserved. Except for the quotation of short passages for the purpose of criticism and review, no part of this publication may be reproduced, stored in a retrieval system or transmitted, in any form or by any means, electronic, mechanical, photocopying, recording or otherwise, without the prior permission of the publisher.

ISBN-13: 978-1-5095-6446-0

A catalogue record for this book is available from the British Library.

Library of Congress Control Number: 2025930184

Typeset in 11 on 14pt Warnock Pro
by Fakenham Prepress Solutions, Fakenham, Norfolk NR21 8NL
Printed and bound in Great Britain by CPI Group (UK) Ltd, Croydon

The publisher has used its best endeavours to ensure that the URLs for external websites referred to in this book are correct and active at the time of going to press. However, the publisher has no responsibility for the websites and can make no guarantee that a site will remain live or that the content is or will remain appropriate.

Every effort has been made to trace all copyright holders, but if any have been overlooked the publisher will be pleased to include any necessary credits in any subsequent reprint or edition.

For further information on Polity, visit our website:
politybooks.com

Contents

Acknowledgements vi
Note from the author ix

Introduction 1
1 Catching Clouds 19
2 The White Witch 38
3 The Sex Witch 64
4 The Nature Witch 87
5 The Death Witch 109
6 The Techno Witch 133
7 Reclaiming the Witch 154

References 166
Index 179

Acknowledgements

This book has been a long time in the making, and I wish I had the space to thank every single person who has been part of the journey. To begin, I'd like to acknowledge my wonderful editor Karina: thank you so much for believing in this book and in me, for helping me find my voice and the courage to tell my story. I'm so grateful for your thoughtful and careful guidance throughout this process.

This book is also the result of so many other people who work at Polity or were contracted through the publisher, who gave me so much of their time and feedback to turn this book into the best version. I would like to acknowledge the critical work they provided: Karina Jakupsdottir (editor), Jonathan Skerrett (senior editor), Emma Longstaff (senior publicist), Sarah Dancy (copy editor).

Thank you to my sweet husband Jathan, thank you for helping this book come to life. For believing in me and encouraging me. For always being up for a celebratory pecan pie. But most of all, for showing me that the kindest, queerest and most joyful love does exist and that I'm worthy of that love. Thank you especially for being the best ghost editor of this book, for always being up for reading early drafts of chapters, author bios and blurbs.

Acknowledgements

I would like to thank my family, for always being there for me, always accepting every new weird thing. I am so lucky to know that home is a safe place for me, and while I haven't always felt comfortable being myself in the outside world, I know that I can count on my wonderful mum, dad and sibling to love and celebrate me in all my wackiness (and frankly theirs too). An extra big thank you to Beau for reading chapters and always being free for trauma dump chats.

A big heartfelt thank you goes to my late Aunty Liz. I wish you could read this book. Growing up, I looked up to you so much. Not only did you give me my passion for reading, you also introduced me to the world of the witch through all the classic pop culture witches of the 1990s: *Practical Magic*, *Charmed*, *Buffy* and *The Craft*. I love you and I miss you so much.

Thanks go to my friends, whom I have been lucky enough to have met and grown up with over the years. Unfortunately, I can't name you all, but I love you so dearly – the TMC crew, the Peak crew and the L9 crew.

I am also deeply grateful to the two academic homes where I have been lucky enough to conceptualize and write this book as part of my job: the 'ET lab' and CEVAW, both at Monash University. A big thank you to my wonderful supervisors and mentors, Sarah Pink and Asher Flynn. Special thanks to Kari Dahlgren and Thao Phan for their feedback on (very) early versions of this book and for celebrating all the little wins with me along the way. Thanks also to my PhD supervisors Kath and Hedda at the University of Newcastle.

Last, but certainly not least, I am so, so deeply grateful to all the witches, priestesses and maenads I have had the honour of speaking to over the years. Thank you for everything, for inviting me into your lives and homes. This book is not only *for* you, it's only possible *because of* you.

This book was completed while I was a research fellow at the Australian Research Council (ARC) Centre of Excellence for Automated Decision-Making and Society (Project Number CE200100005), and the ARC Centre of Excellence for the Elimination of Violence against Women (Project Number CE230100004).

Note from the author

This book is based on real lives, stories and events. In order to protect the identities of those involved, I have changed people's names, removed identifying details and changed elements of certain stories.

There are discussions of domestic violence in this book that some readers may find distressing and/or triggering.

Introduction

Not many people know this, but Margaret Atwood, author of *The Handmaid's Tale* (1985), is the descendant of a witch. Almost ten years before the infamous Salem witch trials, Atwood's distant ancestor Mary Webster was accused of witchcraft in the colonial town of Hadley, Massachusetts. Mary came under suspicion of witchcraft and was dragged from her home and hung from a tree overnight. Later, her body was cut down and dumped in a shallow grave. Despite being lynched, buried and dug back up, Mary survived the tortuous ordeal – which only made people all the more convinced she was in bed with the devil.

Atwood spent much of her childhood hearing stories about her infamous ancestor from her grandmother. Mary's story of survival and resistance was a source of inspiration for Atwood, and, given the sparse historical details available on Mary Webster, she decided to pen a narrative poem titled *Half-Hanged Mary*, which tells the story of the attempted execution from Mary's perspective. What must it have felt like to be out there all night long? To be rejected by her own community? And why was she accused in the first place? These are some of the questions Atwood attempts to explore in the poem. Through the poem, we learn that Mary lived poor and alone on a 'weedy farm' where the townspeople visited for cures for their ills ranging from warts to unwanted babies.

After Mary is cut down, she is even more feared by her neighbours, but is protected by the law and cannot be executed twice for the same crime. She describes the strange freedom she now experiences after surviving death at the hands of her community. The gossip and rumours that led to her accusation and failed execution became a self-fulfilling prophecy: 'Before, I was not a witch. But now I am one', Mary declares. There's something delightfully revolutionary about a woman deciding to live her life in outright defiance of society, even if this version of Mary only exists in Atwood's imagination.

To live in defiance of society's expectations and rules, that is what it means to be a witch. The poem explores themes that would become essential to *The Handmaid's Tale* (both the book and, later, the television series), including enforcing limitations on independent women, policing women's bodies and punishing women who challenge male dominance. Keen-eyed readers of *The Handmaid's Tale* will have spotted that Atwood dedicated the book to her witchy foremother.

The poem is one of my favourite stories about a witch because, rather than focusing on Mary's goodness or wickedness, the emphasis is instead on the question of power. If we read the word 'women' instead of 'witches', we can start to peel back the layers of sexism that wrap around our common assumptions of what we actually mean when we label someone a witch. At its core, sexism is a system of categorization, one that rests on the ideology that men are naturally superior to women. This categorization aims to scientifically naturalize the differences between not only men and women, but also, importantly, between so-called good women and bad women. Witch hunts are a means not only of identifying 'bad women' but also of punishing them and thereby reinforcing that very thin and dangerous line that separates good and bad women. As philosopher Kate Manne (2017: 125) puts it, sexism wears a lab coat; misogyny goes on witch hunts.

In this book, I look at the figure of the witch through a feminist lens that allows us to comprehend *why* we see witches re-emerge in popular culture during certain periods of time. Why are we seeing more witches in the movies and young adult fiction? Why has #WitchTok taken off? Is it a flow-on effect of the #MeToo movement? Or something else? Why does the world need witches now? Why does the world need witchy feminists? These are the questions that animate this book.

My own fixation with witchcraft and feminism began when I was quite young, beginning, unsurprisingly, with pop culture classics like the 1993 film *Hocus Pocus*. I always found myself rooting for the witches who were supposedly the antagonists rather than the intended heroes of the story (but seriously, with Bette Midler singing her heart out and Sarah Jessica Parker's *super sexy* solo performance, how could I not be on their side?). It's very possible that this movie also heralded my burgeoning queerness, on top of my interest in witchcraft and feminism. Later, I would figure out just how interconnected these three vectors of my identity were, which is something I explore in this book. I think that the witch has always helped me to orient myself in the world, to figure out where I belong. As a young, brown, knobbly-kneed kid in an almost all-white school, I wasn't white enough physically or culturally to fully feel like I belonged. And when I would visit my cousins, I couldn't speak our language, and so I didn't quite fully fit in that world either.

I think because I've always felt like I'm part of two worlds and at the same time not enough for either of them, I belonged to the world of the witch the most.

Witches, women and power

What exactly is a witch? The story of the witch does not begin with Mary Webster or indeed with any of the women who were accused of witchcraft during the Salem witch trials. However, that period of accusation and violence offers us a number of critical clues for understanding how we ended up with our current socially agreed-upon image of what constitutes a 'witch'. The *Oxford English Dictionary* gives us the following definition: a person (in later use typically a woman) who practises witchcraft or magic, especially of a malevolent or harmful nature.

Before the fifteenth century, the term was relatively gender-neutral, used to refer to practitioners of magic whether they were men or women. Witches for a long time simply referred to '*somebody* [my emphasis] who causes harm to others by mystical means' (Hutton 2018: 99). The etymological root of the word witch is from the Old English *wicca* (masculine) and *wicce* (feminine). In the lead up to and during the European witch trials (fifteenth to seventeenth century), a shift occurred whereby the term *witch* came to be associated with women – evil women, to be specific (Gibson 2023). *The witch is a woman.*[1]

Why did the figure of the witch change, to refer to women who cause harm via magical means? The short answer is power. Several important social and political changes occurred during the period of the witch hunt, from the end of feudalism and rise of capitalism in Europe (Federici 2004), to major shifts and splits in the Church. The latter changes resulted

---

1 I want to be crystal clear. I do not personally believe that the witches are always women or that the witch is equivalent to a woman. Rather, I want to draw attention to the ways witches have been framed as feminine and explore the sociopolitical and historical reasons for this connection.

in the Church taking extreme measures in order to maintain and extend its power during this period of social unrest and change. A major part of this new political project involved identifying and expelling threats to the power it held, which, in the fifteenth century, meant executing heretics. Pope John XXII in the papal bull released in 1326 declared witchcraft to be heresy, and thus it could be tried under the Inquisition. By definitively marking witchcraft as heretical, the figure of the witch came to be seen as a tangible threat to Christian society that had to be stamped out. *The witch is a threat.*

A threat to whom, exactly? In the infamous witch-hunter manual *Malleus Maleficarum* (also known as *The Hammer of Witches*) Heinrich Kramer writes that 'all witchcraft comes from carnal lust which in women is insatiable' (Mackay and Institoris 2009). If we consider the larger social processes unfolding during this period of time, then this framing of women's sexuality does have its own particular logic. For example, if we follow Federici's (2004) hypothesis that the witch hunts served to create and enforce a newly established role in society for women, one in which women are consigned to unpaid reproductive labour, then this framing of women's sexuality as being out of control and requiring discipline makes more sense.

Simply put, to keep women in their place as homemakers and mothers, the institutions that benefit from this unpaid labour needed to create a system of rewards and punishments. The reward: you get to live in the new world. The punishment: you die in the old world and serve as a reminder to other women about what happens when they step out of line. Witches have a long history of being labelled as sexual creatures. Kristen Sollée (2017) posits that the 'slut' is in many ways the 'witch' of the twenty-first century. *The witch is a slut.*

At first, witchcraft accusations were not specifically directed against women; over time, however, this changed. While both men and women may have been accused, 80–85 per cent of those prosecuted were women (Levack 2015). There are many theories about why women were prosecuted and executed more than men during this period. I've distilled a few of the more popular ones below:

- Feminist-Marxist scholar Silvia Federici (2004; 2018) argues that the witch hunts were a means of stripping women of reproductive control, constructing and subsequently imposing a gendered and uneven division of labour and capital.
- Historians Barbara Ehrenreich and Deirdre English (2010) argue that the witch hunts were primarily aimed at midwives and healers, as a means of taking the knowledge and power accumulated by women and handing it over to male doctors.
- Witch hunts are an example of a moral panic. Sociologist Stanley Cohen explains that societies undergo periods of moral panics wherein a person or group of people become defined as a threat to societal values; that 'societies appear to be subject, every now and then, to periods of moral panic. A condition, episode, person or group of persons emerges to become defined as a threat to societal values and interest' (1972: 9).
- Archaeologist and folklorist Margaret Murray (1921; 1931) proposed that witchcraft today was part of an ancient fertility cult dedicated to the goddess Diana. She posited that the cult was found throughout Europe in witch sects or covens.

The fourth theory became immensely popular amongst first wave feminists[2] and ended up forming many of the beliefs

2 I use the terms 'first wave feminism' and 'second wave feminism' as a shorthand for describing stages of feminist thought, while acknowledging the limitations of these concepts and their tendency to oversimplify feminist histories.

about witches that we see in both popular culture and amongst witchcraft practitioners themselves. For example, the belief that covens are made up of thirteen members came from her work, as well as the belief that witches could be 'baptized' into the cult or that witchcraft is passed down through hereditary lines. *The witch is not alone.*

A core belief that emerged from Murray's work is the idea that witches have existed for thousands of years, practising their craft peacefully for the good of the community. For example, in her book *The God of Witches* (1931) she argued that members of the cult were persecuted during the Middle Ages and, after their covens were discovered and subsequently targeted, decided to form an underground resistance against the Church and the state. *The witch is a survivor.*

Murray's theories formed the basis of what is often called 'contemporary witchcraft', which was initiated in England by prominent figures including Aleister Crowley, Gerald Gardner and Dion Fortune. These contemporaries are defined by historian Ronald Hutton (2017: 7) as 'practitioners of a particular kind of nature-based Pagan religion; or as a symbol of independent female authority and resistance to male domination'. Inspired by the symbol of the witch, numerous feminist groups during both the first and second wave of feminism took on the challenge of reclaiming the witch from its negative stereotypes. *The witch is a symbol of resistance.*

Witches and feminism

It's 1979 and I'm sitting in a park in San Francisco. The sun is shining and over the hill I notice a group of people dancing with total abandon, their joyful voices carrying over to me on the wind. I find the courage to approach them and they tell me they are celebrating the Sabbat. Surprised and also intrigued, I ask them where I can find out more and they tell me to check out a local feminist bookstore. The bookstore looks cosy and inviting, the walls are papered in colourful flyers with a variety of messages and groups: 'Alone we are powerless, together we are strong!' 'The Obnoxious Wimmin's Network', 'Lesbian Sisters Unite!' and 'Susan B. Anthony Coven #1 accepting initiates (Women only)!'. The last flyer captures my attention and one of the feminist bookstore owners who notices me reading the flyers asks, with a friendly grin: 'Let me know if you want to know more?'

'Who is Zsuzsanna Budapest?' I ask. 'Oh she's amazing', she says enthusiastically; 'she runs a women's only coven in the Bay area, but she's always so busy it's hard to catch her. She works in the first Women's Center, the first of its kind in the States, and', she adds, 'she helped start the Take Back the Night marches. Here's one of her books actually', she said, handing me a copy of *The Holy Book of Women's Mysteries* (1980). 'Actually', she says with a grin, 'if you're interested in this topic we also have a few copies of *The Spiral Dance: A Rebirth of the Ancient Religion of the Great Goddess*'.

Looking at the cover, I feel an inextricable tug deep in my gut. While I hadn't planned on picking up any books today, it looks like I will be heading home with quite the library. 'Who is Starhawk?' I ask, looking at the author's note.

'Well Zsuzsanna Budapest trained Starhawk and now she started her own group with Diane Baker called Reclaiming Witchcraft – we've got one of their posters around here somewhere', the bookstore owner replied. 'Ooh and one last book I think you'll like, she's witchy but also an anthropologist, so the book is more about her research' – and she handed me a copy of *Drawing Down the Moon: Witches, Druids, Goddess-Worshippers, and Other Pagans in America Today*, by Margot Adler. Flipping the book open to a random page, I read:

> The Witch, after all, is an extraordinary symbol – independent, anti-establishment, strong, and proud. She is political, yet

spiritual and magical. The Witch is woman as martyr; she is persecuted by the ignorant; she is the woman who lives outside society and outside society's definition of woman. (Adler 2006: 183)

Full transparency: I was not alive in 1979. However, I do often wonder what it would have been like to be alive during that time. Not only were there burgeoning witchcraft and pagan groups popping up all over, not just in San Francisco but all over the States (as Adler documents in her book), there were also second wave feminist activities unfolding, gay rights groups forming and marching and vehement eco-activist protests under way. For example, 'during this period, many (Reclaiming) Collective members and people from the larger Reclaiming community were prominently active in anti-nuclear civil disobedience in such places as Lawrence Livermore Lab and Diablo Canyon' (M. Macha NightMare and Vibra Willow 2002). In an article about the *Origins of Reclaiming*, M. Macha NightMare and Vibra Willow (2002) argue that, 'unlike most other Craft traditions, including one of its foundations, Faery Tradition, Reclaiming has always espoused a connection between spirituality and political action'.

Like Margot Adler, I am also an anthropologist and a witch and I am grateful to her for paving the way for me to undertake research with my own community. I agree with her definition of the witch in part, I think she is an extraordinary political symbol. However, on the last point I must disagree. I don't think the witch lives outside society; rather, she lives on the margins of society, in a sense *she is the margin*, the liminal space between what is civilized and uncivilized. What is tame and what is wild. She is still part of society because she herself is a boundary object. The witch is the line women cannot cross lest they be rejected by their own society. She is not necessarily 'outside society's definition of woman', as Adler would suggest. I would argue that *the witch is integral to how we define and control women as a society.*

Modern witchcraft could be seen as an attempt to reclaim the witch from this bind. A core part of the mission of the Reclaiming tradition that Budapest and Starhawk co-founded is to empower women to 'reclaim their authority/power within both domains: to re-form the structures of domestic life (division of labour, parenting, the marriage contract) and celebrate their reproductive capacities as life affirming and sacred' (Salomonsen 2002: 35). Similarly, in her study of witchcraft during the 1980s in England, Tanya Luhrmann observed feminist covens 'talk about witchcraft and "woman's spirituality", as the only spirituality in which women are proud to menstruate, to make love, and to give birth' (Luhrmann 1989: 52). Rituals that focus on sacralizing the body, from celebrating a young woman's menarche (i.e. first period) (McPhillips 2000), to pregnancy, to birth, became increasingly popular during this era as contemporary witchcraft cross-fertilized (pun intended) with second wave feminism.

However, both second wave feminism and witchcraft from this period have been criticized for reinforcing gender essentialism through their efforts, rather than resisting patriarchy. These rituals then end up reifying biological differences and placing women's value on their ability to reproduce. For example, women-only covens were in part a reaction and resistance to Wiccan rituals (such as the Great Rite) that require a priest and a priestess, believing that the sexual polarity was seen as essential for worship and for performing 'magic'. Women-only groups eschew this inclination to ritualize and normalize heteronormativity by making their groups exclusively for women. In some cases, this has led to trans women being excluded from such groups.

In her study of paganism, Christine Hoff Kraemer (2012) highlights how the more religiously and politically conservative communities may be openly homophobic or transphobic towards those who violate strict gender norms. While Kraemer documents the ways that witchcraft communities are recognizing and dismantling this gender essentialism, there are still forms of witchcraft that reinforce biologically essentialist ideals of women as mothers and nurturers. The core issue here is the assumption that there is a universality to women's experiences, one that transcends race, class and sexual orientation.

What I have tried to do here is provide a broad sweep across the recent history of witchcraft and the feminist movement. It is by no means comprehensive, and the focus of much of this literature is on the so-called 'Western world', namely England and North America.[3] It's important to recognize and cover this history because the values and ideals that were developed and disseminated during this time (especially through the books mentioned during the vignette) have shaped the discourses and rituals in other parts of the world, including Australia where I conducted most of my research.

Conjuring up new methods

When I first told people I would be studying witchcraft, I was met with a mixture of reactions. Some were fascinated by the idea, others scoffed and yet others expressed genuine concerns for the welfare of my soul. Like my fellow anthropologist Kathryn Rountree (2003: 2), who conducted her study of feminist witchcraft in New Zealand in the late 1990s, I kept bumping up against the persistent attitude that 'witchcraft was a legitimate topic for study only if it was witchcraft in some "other" culture'. 'Other' here refers to non-Western cultures.

---

3   Here, I use 'Western' while fully acknowledging the problematic usage of this term that has been thoroughly criticized and debated in broader de-colonial and postcolonial literature (Said 1978; Spivak 1994; Ahmed 2000).

In anthropology there is a long history of studying witchcraft in so-called exotic places like Africa, Papua New Guinea and India. This tendency came from a broader colonial trend of anthropologists treating the East as an object of study. It is only relatively recently that people from these regions have become embroiled in anthropology themselves and began the task of turning the critical lens back onto the discipline itself (Said 1978; Jili 2022). This tumultuous history, combined with the recent interest in studying contemporary witchcraft, has led to a division in witchcraft studies in anthropology, with those studying witchcraft as an explanation for social and environmental phenomena such as diseases and floods on one side, and those studying the more recent social phenomenon of people identifying as witches and creating communities organized around the figure of the witch on the other.

An example of the latter can be found in Lynne Hume's (1997) book *Witchcraft and Paganism in Australia*, which has become one of my favourite pieces of ethnographic research, given it was one of the few that focused on Australia. I read her book during my undergraduate years studying anthropology. Her work set my imagination on fire as I read her fieldwork passages while imagining what it would be like to dance around a bonfire with my fellow witches, its sparks flying high under the light of a full moon. Inspired by the works of Hume as well as other anthropologists, including Margot Adler and Loretta Orion, I join this burgeoning legacy of witches-as-anthropologists studying their own communities.

While my insider positionality granted me a certain level of access to the witchcraft community in Australia, I did not have, as a solitary practitioner aka someone who practises the craft on their own, any existing contacts to reach out to. To meet people and immerse myself in existing networks, I attended 'Pagans in the Pub' monthly events, and attended open invitations for meet-ups and public rituals. I travelled up and down the east coast of Australia, attending gatherings, workshops and witchcamps in Brisbane, Newcastle, the Central Coast and Melbourne. I formally interviewed a total of thirty witches, the majority of whom were young women; however, as part of conducting fieldwork, I also engaged in more informal conversations with witches, before and after rituals, over coffees and late night drinks. While I do not quote verbatim from these conversations, the insights I gleaned from these encounters form part of the ethnography I undertook.

During this period, I also travelled to New Orleans as part of another research project that also touches on similar themes: gender, power and feminist religious authority. While in New Orleans, I spoke to what is called a 'House of Voodoo', which included a priestess, her priestess-in-training, her husband, her son and her son's girlfriend. Although Voodoo and witchcraft are two distinct religious-spiritual traditions, they do share a number of crucial similarities that are relevant for the arguments and themes this book discusses. Additionally, woven throughout this book is my own personal story and journey, which is also a major reason why New Orleans was chosen as a place to study, because it was a place I felt a deep connection to. I shared the experiences I had during my time researching Voodoo with my participants back in Australia which became an important point of connection for us. Rather than approaching my research as a so-called unbiased and detached anthropologist, in this book I use auto-ethnography to situate my own personal experiences within broader discussions about witchcraft and feminism.

Ethnography is a method that studies people in their everyday worlds and involves being hands-on, being part of the rhythms and routines of life. What this looked like in my research was not always as dramatic as dancing around a bonfire under a full moon (although that did happen and, yes, it was definitely a high point for me), it also involved performing chores around the house, playing rounds of Dungeons and

Dragons, watching witchy movies and even sharing memes on social media. Ethnography is also a genre of writing that draws on this fieldwork and immerses the reader in the everyday lives of the people using sensory detail and storytelling techniques alongside objective description and traditional interviews. More often these days, ethnographers choose to use a first-person perspective in their writing to acknowledge their presence as both observer and active participant in the culture they are studying.

This book uses auto-ethnography to further disturb the assumption of a distanced researcher 'over here' and their participants 'over there' in the field from whence they return and write about. Auto-ethnography allows me to draw on my own lived experiences and connections to the topic. My personal perspective as a witch *and* as an anthropologist shapes the viewpoint of the book in its entirety. Just as the witch is a boundary object that disturbs social order, auto-ethnography similarly threatens the insider–outsider researcher dichotomy. My auto-ethnographic writing draws heavily from Black and queer feminist theorists to study their own experiences from Voodoo (Hurston 1938), to discrimination in academia (Ahmed 2017), to independent porn (Stardust 2024).

In this book I draw from a variety of materials, from field note journals, personal diaries, voice notes on my phone, and social media screenshots, weaving them together into an ethnographic patchwork (Günel et al. 2020). I take these materials and analyse them using concepts from what could be called both 'high theory' and what Jack Halberstam (2011) calls 'low theory', which in this case includes girly pop culture. I weave these sources together with the stories from my fellow witches as both a provocation and an invitation for you to experience with me what it means to be a witchy feminist and what witchy feminism could bring to your life.

A note on trauma

Throughout the book, I tell a tale that is unfinished, a story of my becoming and learning to be a witchy feminist, a story that is not straightforward or always happy. The personal story I tell includes my own experience with an emotionally abusive and controlling ex-partner. Aliraza Javaid (2020: 1202) reminds us that 'those who "do" auto-ethnography are opening up closed wounds, peeling them open to re-experience the fresh pain again'. Throughout the book I open up closed wounds from this painful past relationship because they are central to the themes of this book: resistance, misogyny and power. I do think it is important to flag this topic now, so you understand why it was necessary for me to re-experience that pain while writing this book and so you know what to expect as you continue reading.

Witchy feminism

Every age embraces the witch it needs. Right now, the world needs witchy feminists. The witchy feminist is a provocative figure. She is both a provocation and an invitation. I became a witchy feminist, and I write this book as one. You might be one too. Ask yourself: do you cringe when people say that #MeToo is a witch hunt against men? Does it fill you with rage when female political leaders are called bitches and witches? Do you feel your hackles raise when people dismiss older women as hags? If you answered yes to any or all of these questions, you might be a witchy feminist. And I have written this book for you. By naming myself a witchy feminist, I commit myself to recovering the feminist histories of witchcraft.

This book is about what I call *witchy feminism* and it chronicles my own personal journey in becoming a witchy feminist, documenting the mistakes, heartaches and discoveries I made along the way. Second, it takes contemporary witchcraft seriously, which means being critical about it and areas that call for deeper reflection. Third, it looks at feminism itself through a witchy lens. To be clear, I am not saying that all feminists are witches, nor am I making the claim that all witches are feminists. Rather, through this book, I argue that contemporary witchcraft has generative and creative concepts and rituals that are useful resources and tools for feminists that are currently underutilized and, in some cases, devalued and dismissed.

There is a long history of things that women are interested in being treated as unserious, witchcraft being a prime example. This is one of the main reasons I wanted to write this book, because so often all things 'witchy' are dismissed as being unserious. As things deemed feminine or 'girly' often are. This dismissal and devaluing of witches stems from the twin pillars of patriarchy: sexism and misogyny. In this book I draw on philosopher Kate Manne's (2017: 107) definitions of these two concepts, which she presents in her book *Down Girl: The Logic of Misogyny*:

> *Sexism* should be understood primarily as the 'justificatory' branch of a patriarchal order, which consists in ideology that has the overall function of rationalizing and justifying patriarchal social relations.
>
> *Misogyny* should be understood primarily as the 'law enforcement' branch of a patriarchal order, which has the overall function of policing and enforcing its governing norms and expectations.

These two concepts share a common aim, which is 'to maintain or restore a patriarchal social order' (Manne 2017: 108). To achieve this aim, good women must be differentiated from bad women (i.e. witches) and the latter must be punished. The work of feminism, or witchy feminism as I call it, is to reveal and resist the ways sexism and misogyny manifest through the figure of the witch. Throughout the book, I offer an exploration of different manifestations of the figure of the witch, including the sex witch, the nature witch and the white witch.

Chapter 1, 'Catching Clouds', sets the scene for the book, by introducing witchcamps, intensive retreats organized by members of the Reclaiming tradition for witches to gather, connect and perform rituals together. While Reclaiming Witchcraft is technically open to 'people with different experiences, understandings and practices', those who attended the witchcamp I went to were largely middle class and white. This chapter introduces the tensions around gender, class and race that emerge in the chapters to follow.

Witches of colour have not benefited from the liberatory power of the symbol, or from the emancipatory feminist discourse of the witch to the same degree as white witches. Chapter 2, 'The White Witch', focuses on the fuzzy line where witchcraft and self-improvement discourses blur together by focusing on the emergence of 'red tent' gatherings: women's circles designed to celebrate menstruation, pregnancy and menopause. This chapter explores the ways in which the spiritual beliefs and practices of these groups have been transformed into commodities for a market economy.

Chapter 3, 'The Sex Witch', describes a 'sacred kink' workshop and the ways witchcraft can be used to reclaim sexuality from stigma and shame. While there are creative ways to explore how witchcraft incorporates BDSM and kink concepts and techniques so as to challenge the idea that feminine sexuality must be controlled, this chapter also offers a critical take on how some traditions such as Wicca end up reinforcing forms of hegemonic heterosexuality and essentializing women as biological creatures. The theme of essentializing womanhood and 'nature' is explored further in Chapter 4, 'The Nature Witch'. This chapter also explores the types of rituals, ranging from large spectacles to the mundane, that are necessary for creating a sense of connection not only to nature but also to each other, weaving together a sense of sociality and community.

Chapter 5, 'The Death Witch', extends this weaving metaphor to the beautiful, chaotic and magical city of New Orleans. In this chapter I discuss the power and potentiality of gossip as means of resistance. This analysis dovetails into the chapter that follows, Chapter 6, 'The Techno Witch', which documents and analyses the mass online hexes that were organized as a response to the #MeToo figures, in particular Donald Trump, Brett Kavanaugh and Brock Turner.

Finally, Chapter 7, 'Reclaiming the Witch', offers my companion feminist theorists and practitioners who have helped shape my thinking and feelings over the years a set of practical offerings for *doing* witchy feminism itself, from companion texts to rituals to covens.

1

Catching Clouds

Springbrook National Park

It's early spring and I am attending my first ever Reclaiming witchcamp. Leaving the city behind and heading inland towards the mountains and the national park, I am struck by the natural beauty of the landscape. Thankfully, I am able to flag down a taxi driver at the airport willing to undertake the hour-and-a-half-long drive to get to the witchcamp, as it is located deep in Springbrook National Park. The rainforest itself is so dense, wrapping itself around the road we are travelling along. As the taxi driver and I journey deeper into the rainforest, not only does the air become noticeably cooler, but the road also begins to morph into a narrow and snake-like shape, winding its way across the side of the mountain.

Springbrook National Park, located in the state of Queensland, is an Australian World Heritage listed area and forms part of what is called the Gondwana Rainforests. These rainforests contain the largest and most significant remaining strands of subtropical rainforest in the world. They are also the principal habitat for many threatened species of plants and animals.

This is where the Australian Reclaiming community is holding one of its annual camps, called CloudCatcher. The other two camps, WildKin and Earthsong, are held in Sydney and Victoria respectively. The camp is located far away from bustling streets filled with people going about their daily cycle of going to work and buying coffees. It is hidden deep in the rainforest, a deliberate decision and one designed for people to retreat from this cycle. It's no surprise that the Springbrook National Park is the chosen location for this annual gathering. The ancient and seemingly untouched landscape beckoning witches to gather, to connect with one another and with nature.

Witches from across the states and territories load up their cars with tents and sleeping bags and begin the long drive to camp. They are leaving behind their jobs as scientists and school teachers to be closer to one another and to the land. The camp is held deep in the rainforest on the side of a type of mountain called a caldera, which is a large depression formed when a volcano erupts and collapses.

The CloudCatcher witchcamp is fittingly named: upon arrival it's easier to see why, as the caldera looks like it is scooping clouds directly from the sky. The property being used for the gathering is lush and green and heavy with mist; the witches park their cars at the base of the caldera and begin unpacking: grocery bags filled with vegetarian treats, face paints for rituals, offerings and outfits for the upcoming rituals. Within a few hours, the witches of the Reclaiming tradition will begin the first ritual, setting the intentions for the rest of the witchcamp.

By the time the taxi drops me off at the camp, the sun has well and truly begun to set. Looking around me, I notice that the cabins are all dark, and I feel my heart begin to race as the taxi drives off into the night, leaving me standing alone with an almost dead phone in the middle of nowhere. Closing my eyes I strain my ears and catch the sounds of faint laughter and drumming drifting towards me. Following the sounds, I begin walking up the hill.

Everyone attending the witchcamp is squeezed into one single hall, the dancing figures and candlelight inside contrasting with the dark stillness of the night. There are so many people in the space that some of them have spilled outside the entrance. I breathe a sigh of relief when one young witch, Matt, sees me approach and gives me a warm smile, melting my worries away. Matt gestures for me to join, and I slip off my shoes and join the circle of witches.

The hall is quite long. Looking at the tall ceilings and raised stage, I realize that the witchcamp was taking place in a scout hall, which explained the wooden cabins I had encountered upon my arrival. It certainly does not feel like a scout hall, especially with all the decorations, vines twisting into wreaths placed around the floor. The overhead lights are switched off; the only source of light is from the dozens of flameless LED candles all over the place, each of them flickering and casting odd shapes on the walls. One tall priestess with waist length red hair sways and is slowly, rhythmically tapping out a beat on the large drum she has strapped around herself.

A group of three witches step forward to the centre of the room. 'There is a thread,' they announce to the room, 'that weaves through each camp, beyond Australia, through our camp to the camps all around the world.' Slowly they begin to walk around the inside of the circle of witches in the hall, making eye contact with each person and encircling their hands in a weaving motion. The red-haired priestess calls out to the room: 'Everyone join hands please, for our spiral dance.' She begins to beat a slow drum beat to set the rhythm of the spiral dance. As I have no idea what a spiral dance entails, I watch closely as witches join hands and follow her into the middle of the room, each person adding another link to the chain as the line of witches weave their way throughout the room.

As I slowly made my way through the room, making eye contact with each person, which I realized afterwards was purposefully designed through the dance, I saw that there was only one other person of colour in the whole camp. I wasn't completely surprised; most of my reading about these types of gatherings (beyond the Reclaiming tradition) had indicated that they tended to attract white and middle-class individuals. I was curious: how does a large group of people who belong to a tradition of witchcraft with deeply feminist activist roots navigate sticky topics like race? Are the beliefs and rituals practised by these communities truly diverse and inclusive, or does their definition of empowerment and liberation rest on a set of racialized logics?

The elements of magic

It's the first morning of camp and I've woken up tired and sore from travelling the day before. My sleep was broken, not because I was on the top bunk sleeping on a thin rubber mattress, but because I had a fight with my boyfriend the night before. After I arrived at camp, I had neglected to message him to let him know I had reached my destination safely. I had texted him when I landed at the airport, which I thought would suffice; I was starting to get tired of feeling like I was constantly being monitored like a child. I was also sick of being made to feel guilty for doing what I loved. I felt doubly guilty for going into my first Path while tired and distracted.

Entering the Path room, I was delighted to see the priestess from last night was teaching this particular session. At the beginning of witchcamp, each participant chooses a Path to follow through a series of activities that are facilitated by (usually) a team of two teachers. Paths are held for two and a half hours in the morning and are a mixture of 'individual and group work, often including discussions, trance, ritual, journaling, craft and other activities and magical techniques' (Cloudcatcher WitchCamp 2024). If it is someone's first time attending witchcamp, like it was for me, then it's expected that you will attend the Elements of Magic Path.

In their book *Elements of Magic: Reclaiming Earth, Air, Fire, Water & Spirit*, Reclaiming witches Jane Meredith and Gede Parma (2018: para. 2) define the elements as 'the basic building blocks of skills, understandings and practice that underpin effective magic and ritual within our tradition'. These skills can include grounding, casting circles, trance work, breathwork and raising energy. In my particular Elements of Magic Path, I was surrounded by a collection of people attending for the first time (referred to affectionately as camp virgins) as well as more seasoned campers. Each day, we would focus on a different element: earth, air, fire, water or spirit:

> All five elements are always with us. Our bodies are made from this earth, literally from its molecules and chemicals. We cannot live a moment without breathing air. The fiery sun heats our planet enough for life to flourish ... we are continually with water – in our blood and saliva as well as the water we drink and bathe in. Spirit we take to be that animating force within us that links us to Mysterious Ones, to each other, and to all the worlds. We can do magic wherever we are because we always have these things with us and within us.

The fifth element, spirit, according to Meredith and Parma, is what connects everyone to the 'Mysterious Ones, to each other, and to all the worlds'. While rituals are important for individuals' experience and self-expression, they also emphasize their capacity to create a sense of belonging. Kathryn Rountree (2003: 105) argues that ritual is 'a very good way of building community'. Her position about the community-building capacity of ritual draws on sociologist Émile Durkheim, who argues that 'individuals engaged in emotionally charged rituals are frequently drawn out of egoistic self-absorption into a self-transcending and transformative experience of social solidarity' (1915: 317). What this boils down to is that rituals have the ability to take you out of feeling like an individual and you become absorbed into the wider social group participating in the ritual.

Take, for example, the spiral dance from the evening ritual. All members present hold hands and follow the ritual leader in a counter-clockwise motion using a grapevine step (Starhawk 1979). As the leader comes near to closing the circle, everyone turns around quickly and moves clockwise. By continuing the dance in this formation, every dancer will eventually come face to face with every other member of the group. The purpose of bringing everyone together, through holding each other's hands and having eye contact, stems from the Reclaiming imperative to create a sense of community and belonging. During the spiral dance I took part in last night, there was a moment when the inner and outer, individual and collective merged together.

'We are the weavers' was a refrain I heard over and over again during my time at camp. Weaving is a popular and powerful metaphor in Reclaiming Witchcraft; Meredith and Parma describe how Reclaiming witches weave together their rituals: 'They generally thread a number of things (understandings and practices) together or layer them one within another, weaving our magic in a careful – or sometimes spontaneous – tapestry' (2018: para. 2). This process of layering and weaving also involves threading understandings and practices drawn from other cultures and religions. The theme of this witchcamp is based on ancient Greek mythology and gods. In the foreword to Meredith and Parma's *Elements of Magic*, Starhawk poses the question: 'How do we forge a mythology that is truly welcoming, across barriers of race and class, and embraces a diversity of pantheons without falling into cultural appropriation?' What I am interested in exploring is how Reclaiming witches navigate the politics of celebrating and invoking gods and goddesses from cultures outside their own on stolen Indigenous land.

Racial politics and Reclaiming Witchcraft

Witchcamps are community-wide events where Reclaiming witches gather for anywhere from four to six days. During witchcamps, participants stay on site, sleeping in tents or shared bungalows, which enhances their experience of connecting as a community. All sorts of activities take place, including drumming, meditations, dancing, chanting and trances. According to the Reclaiming Witchcraft website, there are twenty annual witchcamps held across America, Canada, Western Europe and Australia.

Most of the camps are concentrated on the east coast of America, with names like Spiralheart, Witchlets in the Woods and Redwood Magic. In Australia, there are three witchcamps, one located up north, CloudCatcher (which is the one I am attending), WildKin in Sydney, and Earthsong, which is located down south in the state of Victoria and which is currently 'on hiatus'.

For various reasons, a number of witchcamps are currently on hiatus. The COVID-related lockdowns obviously had a detrimental effect on gatherings such as these, with teams finding it difficult to reform following the crisis. Others, such as Free Cascadia held in Portland, have been on hiatus since 2018 due to organizational issues, according to their website:

> We are also having challenges navigating differences in intentions, values, and priorities for camp within the collective. Some of the unresolved questions include: How can we be in integrity around holding camp on stolen land? How best do we engage with Reclaiming as a eurocentric tradition that

desires to weave in and be welcoming to other traditions/communities while addressing issues of racism and cultural appropriation? How do we host a camp within a community that has varying experience with self/community work around racism and white domination?

Similarly, another camp called Wild Maine (held in Maine, USA), has been on hiatus since 2019, when a ritual was performed that caused a number of people to become upset, with some attendees choosing to leave the camp altogether. According to the camp's website, the ritual involved 'non-consensual kink and sexual coercion, gun violence, body shaming, and reenactments of white supremacy violence and genocide'. While these two examples are not representative of all the witchcamps, the reasons underlying their decision to pause their activities do highlight a broader problem within contemporary witchcraft, one that goes beyond the Reclaiming tradition: namely, the problem of race.

The Reclaiming Collective's Principles of Unity (2021) does make one brief mention of race: 'We welcome all genders, all gender histories, all *races* [my emphasis], all ages and sexual orientations and all those differences of life situation, background, and ability that increase our diversity.' However, it goes into more detail about its definition and relationship with power: 'Our feminism includes a radical analysis of power, seeing all systems of oppression as interrelated, rooted in structures of domination and control.'

Co-founder of the Reclaiming Witchcraft movement, Starhawk (1979; 1982; 2009), discusses power at great length in her books, where she defines three types of power: power-over, power-within and power-with. Power-over refers to the types of power that are enacted through domination and violence, such as colonialism and capitalism. Power-within refers to a living power that infuses the cosmos and every being within it, the power of being able, of potency and potential (Morgain

2010: 114). Power-with refers to social power, 'the influence we wield among equals' (Starhawk 2009: 9; as cited in Morgain 2010: 118). Reclaiming Witchcraft is a social justice movement that aims to combine two forms of power in order to overturn the forms of power-over that structure the world at present.

I want to come back for a moment to the Reclaiming Collective's Principles of Unity quote above, specifically the part that sees 'all systems of oppression as interrelated'. This interrelatedness of systems of power and domination is often referred to as intersectionality, a term initially coined by Kimberlé Crenshaw in 1989, which describes how race, class, gender and other individual characteristics 'intersect' with one another and overlap. There has been a significant amount of backlash to this term in recent years from the political right, especially in the broader context of 'culture wars' and 'wokeism' (Murib 2020); however, the concept of intersectionality is still quite helpful when thinking about how feminist movements and groups like Reclaiming Witchcraft attempt to approach forms of 'power-over' like racism and colonial violence.

The origins of Reclaiming Witchcraft offer us an insight into why these problems haunt the movement today. During its formative years, the Reclaiming tradition blended together ideas and practices drawn from a number of existing witchcraft groups and traditions, including the Dianic witchcraft taught by Zsuzsanna Budapest. Budapest's first coven, the Susan B. Anthony Coven #1, was founded in 1971 and was a women-only witches' coven. The name of this coven is significant because Susan B. Anthony was an important figure in first wave feminism and led the fight for American women to be able to vote. However, as scholar of gender, race and sexuality Megan Goodwin (2021) highlights in an essay on witchcraft and intersectionality, Anthony was fighting for *white* women's rights: 'Susan B. Anthony is not a liberatory figure for all American women and neither is a Goddess or goddesses imagined as white. This is why our conversations about feminism and witchcraft need to address intersectionality.'

A now infamous example of the vexed issue of race within the witchcraft movement can be found in the open letters shared between Audre Lorde and Mary Daly. In 1979, intersectional feminist and civil rights activist Audre Lorde penned an open letter to Mary Daly in response to her radical feminist book *Gyn/Ecology*. Lorde argues that, while she enjoys reading Daly's work and draws much from her writing, she feels that Daly uses Black women's words (Lorde's included) to dismiss and disempower women of colour by only drawing on white and Western goddess images:

> To dismiss our Black foremothers may well be to dismiss where european women learned to love. As an African-american woman in white patriarchy, I am used to having my archetypal experience distorted and trivialized, but it is terribly painful to feel it being done by a woman whose knowledge so much touches my own. (Lorde 2021: 90)

The letters penned between these two feminist figures and the subsequent public controversy reveals the unequal relational patterns of voice, power and representation between Black and white women. What the letters draw attention to is narratives of white imperialist feminism that universalize marginality and erase racial difference.

What does this mean in an Australian context?

Australia, like America, is a settler colonial project, meaning that colonizers invaded, displaced and murdered the Indigenous peoples living there, and established a permanent society where their privileged status is enshrined in law. I want to emphasize here that colonialism is not only a *historical event* or *series of events*, even though there are many historical events that are important to the settler colonial project. As British-born Australian scholar Patrick Wolfe and author of the 1998 book *Settler Colonialism and the Transformation of Anthropology* famously put it, colonialism is a structure, not an event.

Therefore, in order to understand the racial politics of the Reclaiming Witchcraft tradition, one must acknowledge the very long and ongoing processes of the settler colonial project. Witches in this tradition and others do not exist apart from these processes and structures. If we use this lens of the settler colonial project we can see how certain ideas, practices and rituals either challenge or reinforce colonialism.

The issues surrounding race that are entrenched in the American strands of Reclaiming Witchcraft also emerge in the Australian context, albeit in unique ways. In Australia, colonialism as a structure shows up in a number of distinct ways. Australia's relationship with and treatment of Aboriginal people have historically been, and continue to be, defined by violence and exclusion. Despite publicly self-congratulating itself for being a 'multicultural' melting pot, Australia has an endemic problem with racism – one that is built on what anthropologist Ghassan Hage calls the fantasy position of the 'white person', that is born 'out of colonial history, one that is essentially European'. White multiculturalism, he argues, evades any commitment that 'we are a multicultural community in all our diversity' because 'we' (aka the white nation) only acknowledge diversity when some form of value can be attached (1998: 140). This is essentially the argument that Lorde makes in her letter to Daly: you (i.e. white people) only notice us when you need something. Otherwise, we get packed up in the 'multicultural' box until you need to pull us back out again.

A number of witches directly address the issue of race in witchcraft and the complexities of performing witchcraft on land violently stolen from Indigenous peoples. For example, Raphael Lavallee[4] (who describes themselves on Instagram as a Blak fat queer feminist witch) proposed a workshop titled *A Sacred Round on Stolen Ground: Decolonizing your Magical Practice*, which offered attendees an 'introduction to and exploration of decolonizing your magical practice'. Importantly, she notes that: 'This workshop is not a solution or a quick fix; this workshop's intention is to better understand how colonisation has harmed and continues to harm Indigenous people and introduce ideas on how to decolonise your practices and ally with Indigenous people and causes.' Unfortunately, the workshop ended up not running, but what this event points to is the uneasy relationship between witchcraft and race, between performing spells and rituals for liberation and freedom on stolen lands.

I just want to note here that this is not a complete picture of the types of decolonial work that have been undertaken in Australia in recent years, it's just a snapshot meant to highlight the tensions surrounding race and witchcraft.

I think it's important not to celebrate witchcraft groups as utopian bubbles where issues surrounding race have been solved or do not exist because they somehow sit outside of society. By the same token, it's critical that we do not vilify them as simply white people appropriating non-white cultures and ideas for their own purposes and gain.

As is often the case, the reality is much more nuanced and messy.

Unbelonging

During my time at the CloudCatcher witchcamp I was lucky enough to have some conversations with Fio Gede Parma

---

4 @raphael_lavallee_artist.

about race, whiteness and coloniality in the context of the Reclaiming Witchcraft tradition. In a podcast episode (Queer Healing Journeys 2019), Gede goes into more detail about the topics of race and cultural appropriation within the wider pagan community, highlighting issues around individuals decontextualizing ideas and practices from their culture of origin and repackaging them to be sold in (often overpriced) workshops. Another issue Gede called attention to concerned white people hijacking the cultural appropriation in order to shame other white people. The topic of cultural appropriation is a big one, which I unpack more in Chapter 2.

Gede is a well-known Reclaiming witch and author of multiple books on witchcraft. They were born in Bali and raised in Australia and, as a fellow mixed-race queer kid raised in Australia in the 1990s, expressed several experiences and emotions that I can connect with. For instance, being constantly asked by strangers 'Where are you from?', which is code for 'Why aren't you white?'. Gede captured this poignantly when they said: 'It's a feeling of not really belonging anywhere.'

Not belonging. An outsider. Throughout my life I have had a foot in two cultures and never truly belonged to either of them. In Australia, I was born and raised in a very white neighbourhood and attended a very white school. I was brown and visibly different, but because of my mixed heritage, my appearance gives out a kind of ethnic ambiguity that has led people to ask the same question over and over again ever since I was a child: 'Where are you from?' For me, a worse version of this question is the 'guessing game' people like to play when they try to guess where I am from based on my appearance. This game is never played 'with me'; rather, it is part of the fantasy of the settler colonial project where the white person is positioned in the centre, with everyone else on the margins. The power they hold when they decide to play this game comes from what Hage calls the fantasy position of the white person, where they themselves and their worldview are the centre of the world. Everything and everyone else is peripheral to that white centre.

Not only was I raised in a white neighbourhood, I was also raised in a white Church. I rebelled strongly against my parents' organized religion of choice: Catholicism. I would perform tiny acts of resistance, like signing the pentacle rather than the cross upon entering the Church, or refusing to recite the Lord's Prayer. I detested sitting through those long and tedious hours of mass. I would sit in my school skirt uncomfortable on the wooden pews, stewing in silent rage as the priest took centre stage. I knew that there were at least a dozen women working thankless hours ensuring those masses ran smoothly, making sure the candles were lit, the liturgies were loaded up on the screens and the food was prepped for hungry parishioners to feast upon as soon as the mass was finished. Since a very young age I have questioned and argued with others about these injustices I saw but didn't have the language and concepts to describe: invisible labour, patriarchy, systemic oppression.

I could feel how our family not only looked different but was also treated differently by the community. My mother was born and raised in Fiji, an archipelago of islands with a long and tumultuous colonial history. Between 1879 and 1916, more than forty ships made the long voyage carrying Indian indentured labourers to Fiji. Despite the abolition of slavery in Britain in 1834, the supply and demand of the empire required labourers and, thus, the indentured labour system was instituted. Two million Indian labourers, also known pejoratively as 'coolies', were brought to work on plantations in South Africa, Guyana, Jamaica, Trinidad and Fiji. The Indian labourers, my ancestors, brought their gods, prayers and hope for a fresh future to their new island home.

While my mother left her family's religion, Hinduism, behind when she moved to Australia, the threads of Indian-Fijian religion and culture are very difficult to disentangle from one another. For instance, when my grandmother came to visit us to see how the house building was coming along, she placed coins in the south facing corner of the kitchen as the cabinets were being built. Coins are said to attract wealth and prosperity, by appealing to the Hindu gods Lakshmi and Ganesh. Lakshmi is also the name of the Hindu goddess my grandmother chose for my middle name; her story is a favourite of mine for obvious reasons. In addition to being linked to wealth and prosperity, Lakshmi was born fully grown from a churning sea of milk and honey on top of a lotus flower.

Names are important. In some witchy communities, people rename themselves as a way of reclaiming their identity. I clearly remember when my sister underwent her Catholic confirmation ceremony, one of the three major sacraments of Catholicism alongside baptism and holy communion. One of the most significant parts of the ceremony is choosing your confirmation name, which sits alongside your middle name.

I chose Saint Rose of Lima, to honour my favourite witchy aunt who shares the same middle name. A few years later when it was my little sister's turn to choose her name, she came to me and asked for my advice. At that same time, I was diving deep into the world of Celtic paganism, learning more about the mystical and spiritual world of my father's ancestors. One figure caught my interest: Saint Brigid. Many historians (and pagans) have argued that Brigid was syncretized with the Christian saint who held the same name. Legend says that this was a deliberate move on the part of the Church to encourage more pagans to convert to Christianity. I told this story to my younger sibling, who, like me, was disenchanted with our Catholic school and was quite delighted at the thought of choosing the name of a Saint who was secretly a Celtic goddess in disguise.

Our family is quite 'syncretic' or blended in many different ways. I would eat vegemite sandwiches for lunch at school and dine on chicken curry at night. At the weekends, mum would vacuum while listening to Bollywood top hits and Fleetwood Mac. Straddling these two different cultures and never really feeling completely 'at home' in either is a large reason why witchcraft appealed to me. Somewhere, and a community, where I might find the sense of belonging I craved.

Casting the circle

The first time I experienced this feeling of belonging, the moment where I felt my sense of self, my individuality, dissolve into the 'we', the group, was during the last evening ritual at witchcamp. The Elements of Magic group I had been a part of over the previous three days was invited to open and close the evening ritual for the entire camp, which gave us the opportunity to put into practice the skills and knowledge we had been practising together.

An important and fundamental witchcraft skill is casting a circle. This involves 'invoking the quarters', which refers to the four directions aligned with the elements: north with fire; south with earth; east with air; and west with water. Witches will often place symbols, such as incense and candles (for air and fire, respectively), at each of the quarters in the circle to symbolize the presence of these elements in the circle. Movement around the circle clockwise, or 'deosil', mimics the movement of the sun as it moves from east to west. In this way, the practice of circle-casting – the body of the witch (or witches) walking or dancing – traces the movement of the sun.

Casting a circle is a common means of creating sacred space for ritual work. The reason for holding this ritual outside in an open space is to emphasize a sense of connection with the land. We invited each element using sounds we could make percussively. For fire, we clicked our fingers together, our snaps capturing the essence of ignition, of the spark, the catalysis of fire. For water, hisses poured out of our mouths like a waterfall. For air, we pushed all the air from our lungs with a collective 'haaaaaaaaa'. Finally for earth, one young man in our group fell to the ground, slamming his fists into the earth and emitting a deep and guttural growl.

After inviting the elements into the circle with us, we invited Dionysus to join us. Following our lead, the other witches chanted with us: 'Io Zagarus! Io Bromios! Io Iacchus! Io Dionysus! Io Evohe!'[5] For those who were not ancient-mythology nerds in high school, Dionysus was a bit of a party animal. He is known as the Olympian god of wine, pleasure, festivity, madness and wild frenzy. He had handmaidens too, called maenads, which translates to 'the raving ones'. Great theme for a witchy gathering, right?

To invite the ancient Greek god Cybele, our small group dropped dramatically to the ground and slid our bodies slowly and sensually onto the earth. Whispering her name, we 'seduced' Cybele out of the earth and into the circle. As one, we stood up and slowly walked back to join the wider circle.

This was the moment. This is when I finally let go, I stopped worrying and thinking and started *feeling*. The heat of the fire and cool dewy grass was irresistible. I felt my body sink down to the ground as years of pole dance training kicked in. I slid my chest onto the ground, arching my hips high in the sky before slithering all the way onto the ground. Pressing my face into the dewy grass, I took a deep earthy inhale. Earth. One of the elements we were inviting into the circle to be with us. To honour through our ritual.

Working within a circle (Hutton 1999) is often used as a means of creating sacred space for ritual work. Keith Richmond

---

5 Zagreus is an Olympian god, son of Zeus and Persephone, and father of Dionysus. Bromios and Iacchus are other names used for the Greek god Dionysus. Evohe is a cry used to exalt Dionysus.

(2012), for example, describes how Wiccan ceremonies take place in circles that can be either inscribed on the floor in someone's home or marked on the earth. In her study of contemporary British covens, Susan Greenwood (2000: 83) observed that 'witchcraft rituals tend to be conducted outside in woods or open spaces; the emphasis is on a connection with the land and its spirits'. This sense of connectedness stems from the desire to live in harmony with rather than separation from nature; in this way, ritual is a means of closing this gap (Adler 2006: 239). Casting a circle to demarcate sacred space from everyday space is important for achieving transformation, which is the primary goal of ritual performances, as Vivianne Crowley states: 'The true purpose of all magic is transformation. This can be transformation of the outer world but, more importantly, it is transformation of the inner world that is the aim' (1996: 200). This sentiment is echoed by Lynne Hume: 'In spite of its seemingly theatrical mode, its tools and paraphernalia, ritual is only a means to an end. Ritual is the outer form whose purpose is to act as catalyst to the inner process ... Neither ritual nor magic are intended to convert the sceptical or astound the novice, but are used as tools to transform the individual' (1997: 143).

This idea of being able to transform oneself shares a similar philosophical foundation to the New Age movement and the human potential movement. Other key characteristics they share include 'a reluctance to over-institutionalize; the recognition of the need for a spiritual idiom in feminine terms; a sense of animism; an emphasis on the non-rational and a belief in reincarnation' (Greenwood 2000: 9). All of the above (with the exception of reincarnation) appear in Reclaiming rituals. I would add to this list the tendency to borrow from and weave together ancient gods and goddesses (like Dionysus and Cybele) into their witchcamp themes and rituals.

However, as I have explored in this chapter, this pattern of borrowing from other cultures and times reinforces the fantasy of post-racial relationality. What I mean by this is that when groups take bits and pieces from different times and spaces, reassembling or re-weaving them into their own tapestry, they move beyond a desire for empathetic recognition towards something more extractive. The notion of cultural appropriation has become more mainstream as of late, but the definition of the concept has become a bit muddled. In the next chapter I explore the fine line witchcraft walks between appropriating the voices and cultural contexts of racialized, fetishized others and recognizing the sociopolitical difference necessary for antiracist feminist solidarity.

2

The White Witch

There is something magical about the ocean at night. Walking along the dark and narrow street looking at the almost identical townhouses, I listened as the waves surged and gently crashed on the foreshore. A little vintage red car slowed down as it went past me and I felt my hackles rise in anticipation until I saw an older woman, full figured like the Venus of Willendorf, lean out the side of the driver's window and call out: 'Are you going to the red tent gathering?' A young man turned around to answer and she snapped at him: 'Not you.' Slightly intimidated by her demeanour, I sheepishly nodded: 'Yes, this is the house.'

Walking through the claustrophobic hallway, I am greeted by a very affectionate Dobermann, who was clearly thrilled at the number of guests coming through who were willing to give belly scratches. I knelt down to concede to her wishes and took in my surroundings. The house had such a distinctly witchy vibe; Willow was clearly comfortable expressing this side of herself. I felt a twang of jealousy. My boyfriend would never let me have a large bookcase full of dried herbs and witchy books and painted drums in our house.

Willow wasn't much taller than me, with tight grey curls framing her face. Her cheeks were pink from walking up and down the stairs ferrying her guests to the backyard. Her eyes crinkled and the lines around them spread as she came close to embrace me. As she enveloped me in a hug, I noted that witchy folk hug differently from regular folk: they squeeze more tightly and the embrace tends to last longer. Taking my hand, she guided me downstairs through the kitchen where her husband and son sat at a scrubbed and well-loved timber table. Stepping into the backyard, I saw I wasn't the first to arrive; several women were already gathered around a small fire-pit chatting to one another.

Before coming along to this event, I had borrowed a copy of *The Red Tent*, the book that inspired this gathering and hundreds of others like it across Australia, America and the UK. Anita Diamant, an incredibly influential radical feminist, published *The Red Tent* in the late 1990s, retelling stories that were popular in many witchy and pagan circles. Set in a historical and biblical context, Diamant imagines a world where women do not fade into the background. The focus of her book is on the biblical character of Dinah, daughter of Jacob, who was raped by Shechem, son of Hamor the Hivite. Dinah's story is one that is deeply bloody and violent. Like so many characters who are used in rape narratives as plot devices, Dinah is essentially voiceless. Her identity is created through the violence enacted against her body.

Diamant tells the story through Dinah's perspective not only to give her a voice, but also to layer her character with nuance and depth. It is through her eyes that we experience everyday life and rhythms of women's activities like cooking, cleaning and weaving. Most importantly, the reader experiences the magic of the red tent. The red tent is a space where women are secluded when they are menstruating, to rest and have time away from their normal activities. It is also where women give birth and share the knowledge of midwifery and childrearing. As a space that is demarcated from the more mundane facets of everyday life, the red tent takes on a sacred quality. Within this sacred space, the women undergo rites of passage through the various stages of womanhood. In particular, it is where they gather to reify and renew their bonds as sisters, as friends, as daughters and as mothers.

The idea of the red tent proposed in Diamant's retelling ignited a movement, with red tent gatherings popping up all over the United States, parts of the UK, even in Australia and New Zealand. Inspired by the book, these groups aimed to create a sacred space for women to rest and care for one another. Crucially, the 'red' in the red tent signifies menstrual blood – the other core value and purpose of the gathering is to challenge the idea that menstrual blood is dirty, something to be ashamed of, hidden, stigmatized. In this chapter, I begin by exploring why it's important to challenge the stigma around menstruation in the first place. I dig deeper into these subversive practices and unpack some of the ways they, on the one hand, attempt to subvert these taboos through their practices and, on the other, commodify spiritual practices from other cultures and religions. While the intentions of these groups come from a social justice perspective, when put into practice, they spiritualize the worst aspects of predatory capitalism.

Blood magic

Before we dive into menstruation rituals, I think it's important to address the red elephant in the room – namely, why do we need menstruation rituals in the first place? Given that there are tampon and pad advertisements on television and all over social media, can we even really say that period taboos still exist? A taboo is a symbol of an invisible agreement within a community, something that implicitly maintains the social order. An (extreme) example would be one around eating meat: animal meat is fine, but consuming human flesh is taboo. A lot of social taboos focus on acts that are fleshy and fluid in nature, like adultery.

Common period taboos are centred around the idea that women are impure, dirty or sinful while they're menstruating. In the West, the vast majority of the messages and norms are constructed around the belief that menstruation should remain hidden. This belief has a long history, stretching back to the Bible. An oft-cited example of menstrual taboo is in Leviticus 15:19–33, a passage that asserts that women (along with anything they lie or sit on) become 'unclean' during menstruation. If a non-menstruating person touches either the menstrual blood or anything the woman has touched, they too will become unclean.

These myths go back even further. In ancient Rome, Pliny the Elder argued that menstrual blood contained powers with no limit. Natural catastrophes such as hailstorms, whirlwinds and lightning were said to be driven away by a menstruating woman (Barney et al. 2006). Menstrual blood was also said to sour crops, wither fruits and vegetables, kill bees, drive dogs insane, dull the brightness of mirrors, blunt razors, turn linens black, and rust iron and bronze. Ancient Roman writer Columella tells us that a menstruating woman could kill a young plant by merely looking at it.

Those who menstruate have always been thought of as powerful; the taboos constructed around periods are designed to control this power. While there are many examples of how periods and those who menstruate are demonized, seen as a threat to the social order, there are also instances where period blood (and therefore those who menstruate) are seen as something special, to be revered.

This reverence comes from menstruation's long association with the moon, more specifically, the synchronization of period cycles with lunar cycles. Even the etymology of the word draws this connection: menstruation comes from the Latin *menstruare*, meaning monthly, stemming from the Greek *mene*, meaning moon. In Mayan mythology, menstruation came from the moon goddess whose monthly blood was a punishment for having sex with the sun god (Braakhuis 2005). According to the stories, her blood was stored in thirteen separate jars, where it transformed into snakes and poison to be used in various potions. Menstrual magic, or blood magic, has a long and colourful history intertwined with magic and nature.

Magic and witchcraft are often used synonymously. However, the two terms have quite different origins and meanings. Since I already covered witchcraft in the Introduction, I'm going to focus here on magic. Magic (sometimes spelled magick) is the practical application of rituals or actions underscored by a belief that the individual or group can manipulate natural forces and/or beings. Aleister Crowley (1875–1947), a British occultist, defined 'magick' as 'the Science and Art of causing Change to occur in conformity with Will' and added the 'k' in order to distinguish ceremonial or ritual magic from stage magic.

From the twentieth century onwards there was a rise in the use of the label of 'white magic' (Davies 2007). More recently, according to sociologist Douglas Ezzy, the term 'white witchcraft' has been popularized by literature aimed at the consumerist mass market. White witchcraft, he argues, 'has been deliberately reshaped for consumer capitalism' using the moniker of 'white' to appeal to a more general audience unfamiliar with witchcraft (2006: 17). Ezzy suggests (and I agree) that white witches are not feminist, they don't question or challenge contemporary attitudes towards sexuality, they don't raise concerns about the environment. Essentially the 'white' in 'white witch' is used to separate good (white) witchcraft from bad witchcraft. I use white witchcraft as Ezzy does, to describe a type of witchcraft shopped by and for consumption.

However, I add another layer to complicate this definition, because I define this type of witchcraft not just as 'white' as in good, but 'white' because it is made by and packaged for white women. The type of blood magic, aka menstrual magic, that I describe in this chapter complicates this definition of white witchcraft because the women who participate in the red tent gatherings are in fact participating in rituals that question socially accepted norms regarding women's bodies and sexuality, by specifically targeting menstrual taboos.

Beyond this small group of women, interest and online discourse about menstruation has surged. On TikTok, #lutealphase has more than eighty million views, with thousands of videos demonstrating 'How to Use Cycle Syncing to Connect with Your Body'. Cycle syncing, put simply, involves changing your diet, exercise routines and other lifestyle habits based on your menstrual cycle. While the research on the subject of menstruation in general is scarce (as is most research regarding women's bodies – *thanks* medical sexism) the idea has a chokehold on the fitness industry right now. On the one hand, I think having public discussions about periods that do not shame or vilify women's bodies is an important and necessary step in the right direction. On the other hand, there is every chance that this is just another 'biohacking' fad being used to shame and control women in new and different ways. For example, women describing why they 'feel ugly' during their luteal phase, and other videos circulating with men timing their sexual advances depending on their partner's cycle. Gross. Again, rather than breaking out of the ties that bind, we just end up making the same mistakes and tying women's value back to their bodies, whether the focus is on their attractiveness or their relative 'energy output' for a workout.

But does this actually increase the visibility of menstruation? I'm not convinced. Keeping periods hidden is part of the social contract, to maintain social order. Breaking that contract requires women to bring menstruation into the open. But what does that look like in practice? In the art world, 'menstrual art' has its own category. In 2023 and 2024, a museum in Berlin ran 'Flow: The Exhibition on Menstruation',[6] which included a whole series of installations covering everything about menstruation, from periods in pop culture to the 'history of undergarments and menstrual products'. It also looks like #bloodmagic on TikTok, with popular videos demonstrating how to use your period blood to bind a lover to you. What Willow and her friends were practising seems to sit somewhere between challenging menstrual taboos and creating a new form of spiritual consumer capitalism.

New Age Tupperware parties

Sitting around the fire together, I could see how the story of Dinah had inspired Willow to try and recreate this type of space in her own backyard. She described to us in detail some of the red tents she had set up and run in the past. 'We had bolts of cloth in every shade of red you can imagine rolled out on the ground and surrounding us, sweeping up to the top of the tent', she described. 'We had cakes and delicious fruits like apples and pomegranates spread out everywhere in the most decadent feast.'

This all sounded quite idyllic, but while I was intrigued by the idea, I felt ill at ease. I also felt uneasy as the only person of colour present. Which wasn't necessarily an unusual experience for me. Yet, here we were, a group of witchy women gathered on settler colonial land, LARPing an empowerment fantasy of an Arabic woman who was the victim of rape. Spiritual practices have an uncanny ability to flatten

6 https://www.smb.museum/en/exhibitions/detail/flow-the-exhibition-on-menstruation/.

cultural differences, smoothing out these violent details into a comforting red scarf that can be wrapped around one's shoulders.

Contemporary witchcraft has been heavily influenced by other spiritual movements, including New Age spirituality.[7] I sensed that this is what was happening here, an eclectic re-mixing of self-help pop psychology with healthy servings of exotic stories and practices for some flavour. This was confirmed when Willow passed around a bowl of 'potions', herbal sprays, for us to smell. She explained that this was a carefully selected collection of women-specific potions. I noted that she waited until much later into the evening to offer the 'potions' for us to experiment with and, if we wanted to later on, buy from her. Smart move: too early and it would have seemed odd, but she was clearly experienced at selling this particular product.

She had carefully curated this audience, choosing women who were interested in 'doing the work' (a common self-help phrase), dealing with various hardships (like divorce and domestic violence) and, crucially, having an active interest in spirituality. What I found striking was how effortlessly she wove together stories about women coming together and rediscovering sisterhood and undoing feelings of shame around their bodies; and, in the same breath, selling us overpriced and watered-down essential oils. One brand of essential oil, doTERRA, caught my attention as it had been gaining rapid popularity and media attention. doTERRA is a wellness company that offers people, mostly women, opportunities to work from home, be social and find economic

---

[7] I should note that, although witchcraft has a lot in common with, and many ties to, the New Age movement, there are also critical points where they diverge, and there are many witches who would baulk at the idea of being associated with or labelled as New Age.

freedom. Not unlike the Tupperware parties you might remember your mum hosting: mine certainly did.

Despite doTERRA's commitment to 'improve the lives of the communities' from where they extract the ingredients for their essential oils, according to the official website, a 2023 piece published in the *Guardian* (Fobar 2023) reveals a much less shiny happy people picture. A two-year investigation revealed that women working for doTERRA's frankincense supplier, a Somaliland company called Asli Maydi, are not experiencing 'improved lives'; rather, they are 'living a life of hell'. The women are employed by the company to sort frankincense resin used to make one of doTERRA's most expensive oils. They are severely underpaid and work in incredibly harsh conditions with no breaks, no running water and no toilets. To top it all off, the company is led by a politically powerful man who has been accused by numerous women of sexual assault.

According to the piece in the *Guardian*, in 2020 the Somaliland government introduced a regressive new bill that would enable women to be punished for making 'false' reports of rape. Which means the women have very little recourse to pursue action or justice against those who assault them. Interestingly – and by interestingly I mean horrifyingly – women can also be penalized for using witchcraft to obtain sex:

> Any individual who deliberately casts a spell on a person, with the intention to fornicate or commit zina [unlawful sexual intercourse] with the bewitched, or for a third party to fornicate with the bewitched, has committed a criminal act of witchcraft [for the purpose of] rape. [That person committing the witchcraft] is liable to have the death penalty imposed. (Horizon Institute 2020: 14)

The red tent event I attended freely used the trappings and language of witchcraft, something that women on the other side of the globe could be executed for. Some people prefer to separate 'witchcraft of the West' – i.e. people in places like America, Europe and Australia who practise witchcraft and identify themselves as witches – and people in developing countries – like Somaliland and Papua New Guinea, where witchcraft is an unseen yet powerful domestic and political force. As the journey of frankincense shows, the two are not as separate as one might assume. In both contexts, a multilevel marketing company is relying heavily on women's precarity and labour for their own profit with the veneer of 'empowering' women all around the world.

Wellness brands like doTERRA certainly are empowering in the sense that they are billion-dollar companies, just not for the women sourcing the ingredients or selling the products on the other end, despite the claims they make. The political economy of 'spiritual wellness' products like essential oils, crystals and sage smudge sticks is not removed from the violence and exploitation of capitalism. Kimberly Lau argues that spiritual wellness companies like these deliberately fabricate the image of ethical products so that 'consumers can believe that their purchases are also political acts that help subvert the larger systems of global capitalism. It is precisely this impression that consumer power has some ability to undermine capitalist systems, however, that ultimately allows New Age capitalism to profit and thrive' (2000: 14). Companies that operate within such New Age capitalist logics rely on forms of feminine labour to sell these products, and structure their marketing tactics to leverage women's intimacies and friendships. For example, even though Willow didn't directly call the red tent a 'house party', in many ways her red tent mirrored the types of marketing strategies employed by companies such as the legendary brand, Tupperware. When Tupperware first hit the market, it was not initially successful. It did not become so until the idea of the house parties introduced the product to women's intimate networks.

Alison Clarke (2001) explains that 'the [Tupperware] sales technique thrived on the social obligation generated by women's networks and the impetus toward reciprocity'. The sales technique in question was the 'party model' that heralded the now famous 'Tupperware party', where women – often housewives – would host a gathering in their homes and invite their friends to experience the goods for themselves. The suburban home became a picnic ground for direct sales due to the increase in consumption and a concomitant desire for new forms of knowledge and sociality. The Tupperware party model promised women not only new forms of sociality, but unparalleled forms of independence, empowerment and, above all, entrepreneurialism, at a time when the majority of them had no such opportunities.

Now I should say that Tupperware does not promise those who sell its products that they will reach some kind of enlightenment or spiritual fulfilment. However, wellness corporations like doTERRA prey upon this desire, and exploit the intimacy and trust created in these exact types of contexts. Take the red tent gathering, for example: we were gathered in Willow's house, her home. Everything from the setting, her home, to having her daughter participate in the intimate details she shared about her menstruation, were woven together to create a trustworthy tapestry. Willow wrapped this tapestry around us as she told the story of red tent gatherings and her efforts to resurrect this lost practice. It certainly was an alluring offer – a reprieve from the pressures of everyday life, a chance to gather together for no other reason than to be with one another, to support each other. What's more, Willow believes in this dream. That's the biggest difference between the Tupperware and the doTERRA parties. Sure, you have to believe that the plastic storage containers are going to be a time saver and the make-up will transform your appearance. But you don't need to believe that the containers or make-up are going to help you find meaning in life.

And that's the difference: these brands and their spinoffs have created opportunities for women to find economic freedom. Wellness brands have deliberately cultivated a spiritual dimension to target those who try to find enlightenment through both consumption and the commodification of the self. Willow consumes the products she is selling and commodifies herself in the process of hosting the red tent gatherings. Her home and all its witchy aesthetics, her flowy boho clothes and grey hair all work together to communicate a sense of spiritual authenticity. And it worked. Had we entered a stock-standard suburban house with beige furniture and walls, the red tent gathering would have felt affected and contrived. Which is why these wellness companies embed themselves in existing eclectic spiritual practices like red tent gatherings.

Spiritual self-improvement and self-care

The problem with taking an eclectic approach to spirituality – something I definitely did in the late 1990s; I even called myself an 'eclectic witch' for a while then – is that it very quickly becomes an exercise in extractivism. But when it is done in the name of 'improving oneself' or 'becoming that girl' then, hey, that's alright. This is a distinctly postfeminist way of 'doing' spirituality.

Sociologist Madeleine Castro frames her analysis of red tents through a postfeminist lens that highlights 'individualism, choice, and agency, a focus on women's bodies, regimes of beauty and an insatiable demand for continuous "self-improvement"' (2020: 389–90). I observed this type of language a lot while hanging out with witchy folk in general, and this was especially present the night of the red tent gathering. The individualizing of problems, from divorce to domestic violence, reduces them to the level of individual responsibility, simultaneously flattening and ignoring the myriad structural inequities and social factors at play. This type of spirituality has latched onto the idea of self-care as both a core value and set of feminized practices.

A Google search of self-care brings up images of thin (usually white) women sitting in a lotus pose, surrounded by arrows pointing to various icons that represent various types of activities such as reading, drinking tea, listening to music and exercising. All of which are meant to be done alone. The concept of self-care actually comes from a much more radical and activist school of thought. Radical feminist and philosopher Audre Lorde wrote about why self-care was a necessity not a luxury during her battle against cancer:

> Sometimes I feel like I am living on a different star from the one I am used to calling home. It has not been a steady progression. I had to examine, in my dreams as well as in my immune-function tests, the devastating effects of overextension. Overextending myself is not stretching myself. I had to accept how difficult it is to monitor the difference. Necessary for me as cutting down on sugar. Crucial. Physically. Psychically. Caring for myself is not self-indulgence, it is self-preservation, and that is an act of political warfare. (1988: 130)

That last line has become so well known that it is dangerously close to becoming a cliché. This type of radical political feminism is usually absent from the spiritual or New Age forms of self-care. For example, Willow selling us essential oil 'potions' to help us contend with menstrual cramps is more closely related to the type of self-care that is stripped of its political and radical Black roots. What those essential oils represent is a form of postfeminist spiritual feminism, one where self-care is individualized, commodified and depoliticized.

Given the research that I do on witchy people together with my own interests in all things witchy, my social media algorithms are primed to show me products and services that are precisely in line with this type of thinking. Scrolling in bed one night, I get an ad on Instagram for a subscription to a monthly modern mystic box containing a spring cleansing bundle made from lavender and rose. Those who initiated the concept probably didn't have this in mind when they introduced and developed self-care. The idea that you can subscribe to a monthly delivery of spiritual goods, consuming them for the month and tossing them aside for new products, is not tied to radical activism; rather, it spiritualizes the worst aspects of predatory capitalism.

The fact that the company avoided using the phrase 'sage smudge stick' caught my attention. On the one hand, yes, the 'bundle' was made of lavender and rose so it was technically not a sage stick, but they deliberately chose not to use this more well-known label. I suspected that they had become wise to the criticism around using sage sticks and decided to avoid any controversy by changing both the name and the ingredients. Smudge sticks are a popular tool for cleansing spaces used by those who practise witchcraft or witchcraft-inspired wellness rituals.

Therefore, I wasn't surprised when Willow lit a smudge stick to 'cleanse' my energy before I entered the backyard – aka the red tent. Willow's daughter held on tight to her mother's flowy skirt, too shy to talk to me but curious about what all these strange women were doing gathered in her backyard. To include her in the activity, Willow offered her the smudge stick to cleanse me. Given our height difference I crouched down to make it easier for her and hopefully make myself less scary. It was pretty damn cute I have to admit, her little hand could barely fit around the smudge stick. I watched as Willow helped guide her hand to waft the smoke over my clothes using a fan made from a feather.

White sage, black markets and settler colonialism

The history of smudging is wrapped up in colonialism and capitalism, which is why many witchy groups are no longer using sage for cleansing, opting instead for bundles of lavender like the one in the subscription box, or more common household ingredients like rosemary. But part of the appeal of something like a white sage smudge stick is its unique and exotic status: it's not a mundane kitchen staple like rosemary – it's a *white sage smudge stick*.

White sage first became popular in the 1960s when it was co-opted by the hippie movement from Native Americans and later became deeply entangled with the New Age movement. In fact, a lot of the trends in the wellness industry are simply repackaged New Age ideas and products. The New Age and witchcraft movements evolved side by side, sometimes completely overlapping in places, so it's no surprise that practices from one side would spill over into the other and vice versa. The problem with all these practices being borrowed and shared across movements and social groups is that, during all this movement and exchange, they end up losing their cultural significance and meaning.

Like many colonial settler states around the world, the US was incredibly violent and hostile towards the Indigenous peoples, which included forced conversions by missionaries. A common tactic of settler colonialism is to prevent people from practising their religion. Since the custom of burning white sage – and other plants like cedar and sweetgrass – was considered to be a religious practice (of purification and prayer), it was forbidden by US federal law until 1978. In an exposé published by *Vice*, the ritual of burning white sage continued despite this prohibitive legislation and forceful relocation of Indigenous people. During this time, white sage 'was adopted by urban Indians because it was easy to find', write the ethnobotanists Rose Ramirez and Deborah Small; 'its use then spread throughout Native America and attained a pan-Indian status' (Marantos 2022: n.p.).

After being subsumed by the hippie and, later, the New Age and witchcraft movements in the 1960s and 1970s, smudging using white sage drifted in and out of popularity, primarily used only by the members of these groups. In the context of New Age capitalism, Lau (2000: 7) argues that New Age ideologies look to other cultures, such as Native American religions, for inspiration and rely on 'sentimentalism and nostalgia for a lost past'. Anthropologist Alice Beck Kehoe (2000), for instance, writes about how this tendency for the West to romanticize 'the other' and the 'noble savage' has led to the rise of 'plastic medicine men' who appropriate Native American religion and culture for profit.

White sage smudge sticks are a perfect example of this phenomenon. Since the 2010s, the white sage market has exploded, with everyone from Gwyneth Paltrow to Sephora to Etsy selling smudge sticks. In 2018, major make-up brand Sephora released its 'Starter Witch Kit', which included fragrances, a tarot deck, a piece of rose quartz and a smudge stick made of white sage. Not long after its release, after witches took to social media criticizing the company for turning their religion into a gimmick, Sephora pulled the kit from its shelves. An aesthetic. A costume that could be taken off at the end of the day.

According to Paltrow's website Goop, 'the practice dates back to prehistoric times and it's been used in every corner of the world'.[8] Which is an incredibly vague and broad brush stroke used to paint quite a specific sacred practice. And while, yes, smudging – using smoke to cleanse – is a practice that exists in cultures around the world, for an American celebrity

8 https://goop.com/wellness/spirituality/energetic-detox-how-to-get-rid-of-bad-energy/.

who has created a multimillion-dollar wellness empire to completely ignore the origins is, frankly, gross.

Hollywood has a lot to answer for when it comes to the surge in white sage's popularity. 'White sage has this mystique as being the most spiritual of all plants in the world', writes cultural educator Tima Lotah Link Chumash; 'Hollywood has really picked up on white sage as the go-to symbol for cleansing' (California Native Plant Society n.d.). Native American traditions are often equated with magic. Take, for example, the Twilight series, where certain Quileute people are born with the ability to turn into wolves. All of this is part of the legacy of white Americans and Europeans that trivialises Indigenous beliefs and ceremonies.

Dr Adrienne Keene (2018), an assistant professor of American Studies and Ethnic Studies at Brown University and citizen of the Cherokee Nation, writes that the 'smudge stick represents the deep pain, sacrifice, resistance, and refusal of Native peoples. It represents a continuing legacy of marginalising and punishing Native spirituality.' Keene goes on to say that, 'when our religious practices are mocked through these products, or folks are commodifying and making money off our ceremonies, it's not about who has the "right" to buy or sell. It's about power'.

The threads of power and extraction are deeply entangled with one another, like the roots of the white sage plant. The demand for this magical herb has increased so much that an entire black market for 'wild harvested' – aka illegally poached – white sage has emerged. Anna Kate Cannon (2022), paralegal and citizen of the Choctaw Nation of Oklahoma, writes: '[While] Indigenous knowledge requires harvesting white sage in a respectful way ... poachers cut off branches or rip whole plants out of the ground, taking so many that the plants are unable to repopulate.' As a result of this illegal harvesting, poachers are now going after the white sage growing on nature reserves. Cannon points out that these 'poachers may be marginalized workers themselves, some are undocumented workers from Mexico and South America who, when caught, can be fined or deported with no consequences to middlemen or corporate buyers'.

This is because that white sage being gathered, both legally and illegally, is not meant for Native American groups and their ceremonies, nor is it intended for the undocumented workers from Mexico and South America. It is extracted, shipped, packaged and distributed around the world for white people to consume – white women, to be exact. The white witch, both racially and as associated with 'goodness'. The black witch literally becomes dirt and danger throughout this extractivist process. Feminist and critical race scholar Sara Ahmed (2007: 153–4) writes that 'colonialism makes the world "white", which is of course a world "ready" for certain kinds of bodies', as well as 'a world that puts certain objects within their reach'. Colonialism works hand in hand with capitalism to make the object of white sage readily available for some and hard to reach for others.

Plastic shamans, as well as other New Age spiritual entrepreneurs, continually pillage from other spiritual traditions looking for new ways to market their products. This constant search and remixing is described by Lisa Aldred (2000: 341) as 'fusing together bastardized versions of these traditions' as these 'ransackers of Native American spiritual traditions' combine religious practices with 'self-help pop psychology, as well as exotic blends appropriated from other cultural traditions'. Just like the Diamant story and the red tent gathering, homogenizing elements from a vaguely Arabic tale with Native American smudging. But how exactly does this homogenizing or 'fusing together bastardized versions' of spiritual traditions occur?

Eclectic spiritual extractivism

The insidious and extractive nature of New Age capitalism functions by using a specific type of racial logics. These logics operate under the guise of spiritual 'eclecticism', which encourages cherry-picking ideas, practices and rituals from various religious and cultural traditions. I could call this process cultural appropriation and move on, and this is usually what this type of practice is chalked up to. The phrase or accusation of 'cultural appropriation' is so overused (often misused) that it has lost much of its oomph. Cultural appropriation lacks nuance, and has a tendency to attack individuals over institutions. Eclectic spirituality often masks extractivism.

Instead I prefer to call this a form of cultural appropriation: *eclectic spiritual extractivism.* Extractivism, global development researcher Christopher Chagnon writes, refers to a set of 'self-reinforcing practices, mentalities, and power differentials', all of which combine to rationalize 'socio-ecologically destructive modes of organizing life through subjugation, depletion, and non-reciprocity' (Chagnon et al. 2022). The specific type of extractivism at play here has a strong racial overtone, which is why I use American cultural theorist Minh-Ha T. Pham's term 'racial plagiarism' to describe the process that's happening.

Racial plagiarism is used by Pham (2017: 73) to home in on how 'racialized groups' resources of knowledge, labour and cultural heritage are exploited for the benefit of dominant groups and in ways that maintain dominant socioeconomic relationships'. Racial plagiarism, she writes, 'is never just about being inspired by but rather improving on an unrefined, unsophisticated, incomplete and, most crucially, unfashionable racialized form', reinforcing a system of value in which the originating culture continues to be seen as 'unrefined'.

Racial plagiarism does a lot more work than cultural appropriation to explain how and why white sage has been extracted from Native American groups and overcommercialized by the wellness industry behemoth. The misuse and overharvesting of white sage plays out against a colonial backdrop, with the pan-Indian practice of smudging being taken from Native

American groups by middle-class white hippies, then taken again by middle-class New Agers, and then taken by pagans and witches, and which is now being used by middle-class wellness influencers and, most importantly, billion-dollar corporations. They might be offering love and light, but, at the end of the day, it's an industry. An incredibly profitable one at that.

What's missing in applying the concept of racial plagiarism to this social phenomenon is gender. The wellness industry targets middle-class white women specifically and uses feminized forms of spirituality like witchcraft to do so. Spiritual wellness practices like smudging and gatherings like the red tent are both highly gendered in large part because they are 'dominated by women both as practitioners and providers of spiritual services, and ... entwined with practices and attributes that are traditionally assigned to femininity, such as care, empathy, emotion and acceptance' (Poutiainen 2023: 4). At the red tent gathering I attended, Willow presided as both a practitioner of blood magic (aka menstrual blood rituals) and a provider of a spiritual service, the service of 'making space' for us, to listen to us. Sitting around the fire, Willow explained to us how she would like the evening to proceed. 'As we move around the circle and each of us has a turn to speak, please ensure you do not talk over others which is what I call cross-talking', she explained. 'Instead, I encourage you all to actively listen – this is, try to listen to what the other person is saying without also thinking about what you are going to say after.'

If you think this language sounds self-helpy, then you would be correct. The self-help sections of bookstores are exploding right now with thousands of books and courses online promising to help you release your potential, to help you 'do the work'. To heal. To transform. To be your *authentic self*. Much of this rests on a Protestant Work Ethic, the idea that work is our salvation. There's also a reason why this literature usually sits alongside the spiritual and/or religious book section. If you think it seems like this type of literature and its associated language are having a cultural moment right now, you would be correct. However, self-help intertwining with consumerist spiritualities dates back to the 1960s, which emphasizes individualism and eclectic spiritual experimentation. The current trend in the self-help world is to focus on the self as a project, one in need of continuous care consumption. The trend towards 'wellness' that we are witnessing right now is in large part a rebranding of so-called exotic Eastern religions (like Buddhism and Hinduism – especially yoga) fused with psychology (via the Mindfulness Movement) and capitalism (through the Prosperity Gospel). This explains, at least in part, why a syncretic movement like contemporary witchcraft so easily engages with Wellness.

Red tent gatherings are a form of spiritual self-help capitalizing on narratives and ideas embedded on feminine spiritualities. Now, just because something says 'feminine' does not mean it is inherently feminist (definitely a mistake I have made in the past). In fact, feminists have previously criticized activities like the red tent for promoting more conservative concepts of womanhood and women's roles. By ascribing value to bodily processes like menstruation and menopause, feminine spiritualities like witchcraft can end up 'reinforcing the valorization of women's reproductive role' (Bobel 2010: 92, as cited in Poutiainen 2023: 4). I myself have written about this previously, arguing that witches use rituals and concepts (such as the red tent) as 'a metaphorical project of reclamation, aimed towards reclaiming historical discourses, the body and community structures from patriarchal power structures' (Quilty 2020b: 107). One of the risks of this reclamation project is the proliferation of a type of feminism that, on the one hand, universalizes femininity and, on the other, sacralizes biological essentialism. The premise of the red tent itself rests on the idea that menarche, menstruation, motherhood and menopause are universal feminine experiences.

This issue is not something that is new to the witch community; for example, Reclaiming founder and witch Starhawk has critiqued the 'cock/womb imagery of the Maypole' as a deification of heteronormativity. Relying on biological definitions of men and women essentializes these categories, which are then reinforced by creating 'women-only' spaces such as red tent gatherings or menstrual magic workshops that end up excluding trans women. A local spiritual women's festival came under criticism for not allowing transgender women to attend unless they had undergone gender reassignment surgery. When this was exposed in an email sent to a trans woman, the organization came under massive criticism. It has since readjusted its position on the inclusion of trans women in their festival. The subject of biological essentialism in witchcraft and the exclusion of trans people from spiritual spaces is one I explore more in Chapter 4, 'The Nature Witch'.

Dark thoughts during the new moon

As we were sitting around her fire, Willow invited us to write down the things we wished to release with the new moon. My hand hesitated, unsure as to whether I should write something generic like 'worrying about the future' or something personal and real. Looking around the small circle, I saw each woman with the same face of concentration, and I decided I would not just play pretend, but I would share with the group something vulnerable, something real. Willow spoke to us in a slow and gentle voice as we wrote: 'We need to listen to our bodies when they bleed. What are the nuances of each flow trying to tell us – the colours, the texture of your [menstrual] flow, the type of pain you are feeling – is there something you need to let go of?' I thought about my last period: it had been a lot heavier and more painful than usual. I remembered standing in the shower as the blood flowed freely; the texture was so thick, I was worried I might have had a miscarriage. Funny thing was, I was more scared of being pregnant than having a miscarriage. Mostly because my boyfriend would frequently joke that if I were to fall pregnant he would 'accidentally' push me down the stairs. No matter how many times I told him I didn't appreciate the joke or find it funny, it didn't seem to matter. He just wouldn't listen.

I want to stop being ignored – I wrote on the little piece of paper. Throwing it into the fire I watched as the edges of the paper curled up in the flame, turning black and then finally turning to ash.

A search on Google will give a thousand different rituals for 'letting go' by burning messages on pieces of paper. One I found recommends doing this by clearing your space using a sage smudge stick. It also recommended performing this ritual during the full moon. The meanings of the moon phases seemed to shift depending on the group; in Willow's group, for instance, we were encouraged to write down and burn the things we wanted to release as part of the dark moon, and also to write down what we wanted to invite into our lives as part of the new moon. Anthropologist Susan Greenwood (2000: 129) has explored the significance of the dark moon in her own research of witchcraft and pagan communities. Like me, she observed that the narratives that witches choose to venerate tend to naturalize the moon cycle as a sacred feminine symbol:

> Dark moon rituals have become increasingly popular for women to celebrate and reclaim what is seen to be the most feminine part of themselves. The dark moon is seen to be the time in the lunar cycle when the old moon dies and is then reborn again. The moon is often viewed as feminine in the way that it waxes and wanes, and female witches identify with its rhythms.

It's not surprising then that witches refer to their menstruation as their 'moon time'. One website provides advice on how to sync your 'period to the moon' because of the synchronicity between the length of a regular menstrual cycle and the lunar cycle: twenty-eight days. This is in large part where the idea of 'moon magic' comes from, the belief that women's bodily cycles are connected to the movements of a celestial body like the moon. The website also states that 'some believe that periods should align with the new moon, since the dark-moon phase is so closely associated with rest and withdrawal for self-care'. While the ritual above calls for the individual to isolate oneself and rest (with the idea that this will make one more productive for the rest of the month), the red tent gathering is intended to bring women together to ritualize menstruation.

But why do they feel the need to make rituals around menstruation in the first place? Feminist theorist Elizabeth Grosz gives us a helpful starting place – women's leaky bodies. She writes that women's bodies are leaky, arguing that 'their genitals and breasts are the loci of (potential) flows, red and white, blood and milk' (1994: 207). The fear of this leakiness has led to the creation of cultural and religious taboos in order to socially manage this leakiness. One young woman I spoke to, Brigid, told me about a vivid memory, recalling her experience of what happened when an object closely associated with menstruation was treated as something disgusting and to be concealed at all costs: 'I hate the shame associated with menstruation so much. My partner and his dad straight up cannot handle anything to do with periods or menstruation, [and if you bring it up] they will say "Oh my god what are you doing? What are you saying? Keep that to yourself!"'

Treating menstrual blood as dirty, as matter out of place, as something to be hidden, is not new. Over recent years we have seen major menstrual product brands attempting to tackle this issue – trying to balance the appetite for more socially aware advertisements that simultaneously don't 'gross out' the audience with the so-called dirty menstrual blood.

Anthropologist Mary Douglas (1966) defines dirt as 'matter out of place', meaning that dirt is an ambiguous and contextually based object. What this means is that dirt isn't 'real'; rather, it is something that is defined by where it is found. For example, when Brigid was staying at her boyfriend's house, there was an incident when his father flipped out when he found the end of a tampon wrapper on the edge of the sink. Had he seen a tampon wrapper in the little bin, he probably would not have had such an over-the-top reaction. But because the wrapper was out of place, i.e. on the sink, chaos ensued. Something that was connected to periods, not actually covered in menstrual blood mind you, just something tangentially attached to the notion of a period, sent this man into a spiral. The world is socially structured through various systems and classifications, meaning that we make rules about where things 'should' be and when they cross the boundary of where they should be, they become 'dirt'.

One of the rituals Willow suggested that we could perform on our own during our moon time involved pouring our collected menstrual blood onto the earth, as an offering. 'Or you can squat down and bleed directly onto the earth, if you're hardcore', she added provocatively. We stared at her for a moment, unsure whether she was joking or not. She was not. The idea of bleeding directly onto the earth next to my house in full view of the neighbours was so far out of my comfort zone it might as well have been on Jupiter. But the idea of offering my blood to the land I was living on, to 'feed' mother earth – I could do that.

So a week later, after the red tent gathering, when I saw the tell-tale brown spots in my underwear, I decided to collect and offer my 'moon blood' to the earth. I waited until the middle of my period when I knew I would have enough blood to qualify as 'pouring'. In reality it was more of a couple of drips. It seemed like such a small amount, such a small moment, but it did signal the beginning of something new, a new way of relating to my body. 'The Craft also demands a new relationship to the female body':

> No longer can it (the body) be seen as an object or vilified as something dirty. A woman's body, its odours, secretions, and menstrual blood, are sacred, are worthy of reverence and celebration. Women's bodies belong to themselves alone; no spiritual authority will back a man's attempt to possess or control her. (Starhawk 1979: 76)

Slowly, but surely, through this work I felt like I was reclaiming my body, my voice, my power.

3

The Sex Witch

'Relax everyone, this isn't going to turn into an orgy.' This is Dara, and my first thoughts when I see him – at twilight, in the centre of a circle of thirty men and women in a cosy, heavily decorated room at witchcamp – is how much he looks like a satyr. It's unmistakable, his lean and slender stature. His mischievous grin. In Greek mythology, satyrs are masculine nature spirits depicted with goat legs and a permanent overly exaggerated erection, companions of the god Dionysus. At this workshop, Dara is acting as priestess for Dionysus, where he is holding space in a special area known as the Bower.

The term 'bower' is a curious one; at the time, I didn't quite understand why they had chosen that word to describe this particular space. After the workshop, I discovered that 'bower' is used to describe an attractive dwelling or retreat, or a lady's private apartment in a mediaeval hall or castle, or a shelter (as in a garden) made with tree boughs or vines twined together.

Dara explained to us:

The Bower is a space held at camp for reclaimed sensuality and sexuality. Having been a priestess for the Bower for two years, we really focused on just connecting back to our physical body. You'll look at some traditions and it's very much about reaching a state of higher consciousness and being able to expand beyond the physical form. We do so much spiritual practice that it is important to be physically present in our bodies.

For this witchcamp, the Bower had been lavishly decorated in honour of Dionysus. Heavily embroidered pillows adorn the floor, the boring blue-grey carpet is covered in velvet blankets and ornate rugs. Ivy vines are draped all around, and are tied back to the altar set up in the far corner of the room. The table is adorned with offerings to, and symbols of, the deities the workshop is dedicated to, namely, Dionysus and his maenads – handmaidens who would be driven to mad ecstasy by Dionysus and take part in frenzied rituals, orgies and even tearing men apart.

The effect of the space and its decorations – more accurately, adorations – is effective. I'm transported to ancient Greece, to a lush party with goblets overflowing with wine, tables laid out with decadent food like pomegranates and grapes. In my mind's eye, I see people hand feeding each other grapes as they caress and kiss one another. People are wrapped up in deep embraces, some in pairs, others in groups. Bodies folding into one another, fingers lovingly handing and feeding grapes and slipping them inside mouths. It's a sensual and sensuous celebration of pleasure. A hedonistic fever dream.

Back in the Bower, I was sitting awkwardly upright and next to the window sill, while others were lounging on pillows, resting on welcoming laps, fingers twirling in one another's hair. I notice I'm not the only one who looks a little nervous; sitting across from me are two young women around my age whom I would later learn were called Tiff and Temperance.

The provocatively titled workshop – Sacred Kink – has been designed to educate us on the potential of incorporating BDSM and kinky techniques in our witchcraft practice. While this workshop would not be, *ahem*, hands-on, so to speak, in sister witchcamps held in California the workshops were much more participatory. Dara told us about one workshop he attended where people observed a couple engaging in sexual acts together. It's clear that Dara knows how to hold the crowd's attention: 'While I was watching this couple that I had no sexual attraction to, both of them, but sitting there and watching was this really powerful experience. In society sex is treated as a taboo, something to be done behind closed doors.' I was intrigued by the things Dara was saying, not only the stories he was telling us but the almost dangerous ideas he was sharing with us. The idea that sex might be sacred. That BDSM and kink might have something to teach us vanillas about having better sex. This became a fascination of mine both academically and personally.

How does one go about reclaiming one's sexuality from social conditions of stigma and shame? This was a question I wanted to know from an academic perspective, finding out what types of sexual politics and practices witches used to reclaim their sexuality. But I also wanted to know more personally. My sexual experience in many ways was stunted; it took going to this particular workshop to help me realize the ways I had been repressed (and self-repressed) and open me up to the big and exciting world of sexual pleasure. I was also intrigued by the idea of incorporating sexuality and spirituality together.

I wanted to know whether witchcraft rituals that draw on sexual elements resist gendered norms, or whether they end up reinforcing them. Who are these rituals targeted towards? And how did kink and witchcraft end up intertwined in the first place?

Sacred Kink and the Reclaiming Witchcraft tradition

> Of all the female sins, hunger is the least forgivable; hunger for anything, for food, sex, power, education, even love. If we have desires, we are expected to conceal them, to control them, to keep ourselves in check. We are supposed to be objects of desire, not desiring beings. (Penny 2014: 42)

Witchcamps represent countercultural spaces for challenging social norms, which is where the Bower comes in. The Bower is designed, as Dara said, as a space for reclaiming sensuality and sexuality. He said: 'I'm going to make a bold assumption that we all learned about sex from different places, so, to start off, how about we all share about how we first learned about sex?' In many ways, the Bower embodied all the different types of hunger that Penny lists above: food, sex, power, education and love.

Going around the circle, we shared how we first learned about sex, and I was surprised at how many of us had been socialized with the same kinds of attitudes towards sex and love. When it came to my turn to share, I felt less self-conscious speaking truthfully about my own sex education because, as it turns out, the pre-internet teen magazines did a lot of heavy lifting in this particular area.

I was pleasantly surprised to hear that, like myself, many of the witches in the circle also felt their sex education (including at school) was incredibly heterocentric, focusing exclusively on heterosexual and monogamous relationships. None of us was taught about how to practise safe sex in same-sex encounters, how to navigate jealousy in polyamorous relationships, or how to be respectful and safe towards trans partners.

While sex is not the primary focus of every single Reclaiming workshop or event, it is ever present. This is because sex and pleasure are not treated as taboo; rather, 'sexual intimacy [is seen as a] path to the sacred, not something that should be denied or denigrated' (Salomonsen 2002: 215). Kink, therefore, is just another pathway to the sacred.

But what exactly is sacred kink? What makes it different from your run-of-the-mill kink? And how can kink be sacred? Isn't that an oxymoron? Put simply, sacred kink practitioners intentionally use kink for spiritual purposes. Kink and BDSM, according to religious studies scholar Michelle Mueller, 'encourages a broader spectrum of erotic experiences by shifting attention away from the genitals to other possible regions for bodily pleasure' (2018: 43) – something that is very much aligned with the workshop being run in the Bower.

The different types of workshops and events represent the long history of radical and revolutionary sexual politics of Reclaiming Witchcraft, which can be traced back to its early days. In the late 1960s, the Reclaiming tradition emerged from the San Francisco Bay area of California. Those who lived on the social margins flocked to San Francisco, a radically left-wing city, because of its progressiveness and higher-level acceptance of diverse cultures and identities. The city became a sanctuary for gay and queer folk, as a result of which many moved there in the 1970s and 1980s – so many, that San Francisco became one of the biggest centres of LGBTQ rights in the country.

At the same time, the city was dubbed the 'porn capital of America', precipitating an explosion of strip clubs, adult movie theatres, peep show booths and kinky shops downtown, which led to the creation of the first feminist advocacy groups for sex workers. The Reclaiming Witchcraft tradition was born from the cradle of radical politics in San Francisco, heavily influenced by the growth of the feminist movement and protests, and the rise of sex worker rights and gay rights groups.

All of this was happening in the context of sweeping changes unfolding in the Western world. The pill, for one, gave women access to easy and reliable contraception which also signalled a broader sociocultural shift when it came to the topic of sex. Once relegated literally and figuratively to the bedroom, sex moved into the public sphere. People on television shows weren't just talking about it, they were having it.

During the 1990s, a number of significant technological advances occurred that impacted the rise of both witchcraft (not just Reclaiming) and the BDSM movement. During her time among the BDSM communities of California, anthropologist Margot Weiss (2011) observed how they developed alongside the rise of IT industries in Silicon Valley. In particular, the rise of the internet during this period led to an explosion of 'classes, workshops, organisations, munches, and play spaces' for those interested in BDSM (2011: 54). BDSM and witchcraft practitioners alike began connecting with one another through new media networks, including internet chat rooms and email lists, as well as print media such as newsletters.

In this same time period, from about the late 1990s to the early 2000s, a number of contemporary pagan authors, including Pat Califia (1998), Raven Kaldera (2006) and Lee Harrington (2009), published popular books establishing connections between sadomasochism and contemporary pagan ritual. The connection between BDSM and witchcraft became publicly visible through the programme schedules of witchy and kinky gatherings and festivals such as the annual Reclaiming witchcamps that happen all over the world.

Sex is also something that Starhawk has written extensively about in her books as well as on her blog. For example, in a post titled 'Auntie Starhawk's Sex Advice for Troubled Times', she defines sex as:

> any way people come together in any combination that is mutual, consensual, pleasurable and life-affirming. Sex is lifeforce – whether that life becomes a new being or simply a reason for us older folks to enjoy living. In earth-based Pagan spirituality, sex is a way of experiencing the Goddess (or any

form of the divine you prefer) within – the pulsating, vibrating, untamed passion of life itself.[9]

She differentiates this definition of sex from a misogynistic form of sex used 'to display power, to humiliate, embarrass, possess or control another'. She takes a Marxist feminist position, arguing that the reason pleasure, (especially) sexual pleasure, is denied in society stems from 'economic conditioning that removes value from our embodied experiences of passion, ecstasy and connection in order to control and exploit us'. The types of kinky workshop I attended are not simply spaces for people to analyse this conditioning; they are designed to give people techniques for experiencing the type of sex Starhawk is describing – mutual, consensual, pleasurable and life-affirming.

A not so happy homecoming

I finally arrived home from witchcamp, ready to unpack my bags and the stories I had gathered during this trip. My boyfriend was still at work so I set my bags down ready to perform my now well-practised ritual of washing my clothes, preparing a snack and decompressing with one of my favourite witchy television shows. To my annoyance, the washing machine was full of (his) wet clothes that he had conveniently forgotten to put on the line to dry, and, to top it all off, the fridge was empty. *No relaxing for me today*, I say to myself as I trudge back out to the car.

Despite being physically and emotionally tired from my travels, I hang out his washing and cook us both dinner, wanting to avoid a fight on my first night home in weeks.

[9] https://starhawk.org/auntie-starhawks-sex-advice-for-troubled-times/.

Sitting on the lounge together flicking through streaming channels trying to decide what to watch, I finally plucked up the courage to ask him about trying some of the things I had heard about during the workshops.

'So I had a really interesting time in the field', I say tentatively. 'Mmmm', he replies, his eyes still locked on the television. Touching his arm to gently draw his attention to me, I continued: 'Witchcamp was really full-on but I had a good time, met some lovely people.' Eyes still forward he grunts his acknowledgement without asking any further questions. Determined to have a meaningful conversation, I pressed on: 'There was one workshop I went to where we learned ....' 'You know I don't believe in that witchy shit', he interrupts. Trying not to show how much he's hurt my feelings, I try my best to recover the conversation: 'No, no. This isn't witchy it's more intimate, it's umm', I stammer awkwardly, 'about things in the bedroom.'

Finally he looks at me, eyebrows raised suspiciously. I can already tell that I have broached the subject in the wrong way, his body language is screaming volumes at me – *I am not interested in this conversation, even less so doing something that you heard while doing your witchy shit.* His face wrinkles in disgust, as if I've said something unbelievably perverted and disgusting. As if I've walked inside with excrement all over my shoes and neglected to take them off, stomping filth throughout our home.

'We're not doing that', he says with a cutting finality, turning his attention back to the television. *Well I guess that's the end of that conversation*, I think to myself. Blinking back tears, I say to him: 'You watch whatever you want, I'm going to go read upstairs.' Opening my book I try my best to read, but I'm still upset from our conversation. So often we would have fights like this that do not necessarily get resolved; rather, he shuts the conversation down and we just move on as if nothing happened. At the same time, because we don't communicate, nothing gets resolved and we don't get the opportunity to learn from the conflict; to understand one another more deeply, we avoid the conflicts from coming up in the first place. This was certainly not the first time we had had a fight about the topic of sex; it was actually a constant source of tension in our relationship. This was exacerbated by a number of key factors, the first being that I am a sexual person, the second was that he hated talking about sex. Not ideal conditions, to say the least.

Sitting on my side of the bed, I open my book only to end up staring out of the window, thinking about how we had started out being so loving and playful in the beginning. How, I wondered, did we even end up here? We used to have long talks together, even in the middle of the night if we woke up, we just held one another and talked about whatever it was we were feeling. Our bedroom was a sanctuary from the stress of the outside world.

Looking around the bedroom now, I felt as if I was sitting in a hotel room. Over our years together, the space had changed from one that reflected both of our personalities to one that only mirrored his. Bookcases that once held both of our favourite texts had been emptied; my books now lived tucked away in a spare closet. No pictures on the walls or trinkets from our travels together. Just bare walls.

I can hear him coming upstairs, I could tell from the way he was stomping his feet that he was angry with me. Angry for bringing up the conversation and angry at me for walking away. Sighing to myself, I knew that he would not actually express these feelings directly to me using words. Instead he would stomp his feet and slam doors. Even the way he turned the overhead light off was aggressive. As he settled in next to me, I could practically feel the heat radiating off him, and his demeanour made my insides shrivel up. I wanted to cry. To run away. To do anything but withstand whatever he was about to say.

'I don't think you should be travelling any more', he said. 'Wait, what?' I say, genuinely surprised. 'It's dangerous and I don't know these people you're meeting with, you haven't told me anything about them and I don't know how many of them are men, for example. I'm not there to keep you safe so I'd rather you just stay here. You've done enough interviews now you can just do the rest from home.' *Well if we could have even half a conversation, you would know what my research is about* – I want to say.

'Can you say something?' he snaps at me. 'I don't know what to say', I respond. 'I have a trip booked to meet with people I met at witchcamp, I can't cancel those. I need them for my project.'

'Well I'm just not comfortable with you going to these places, I can't get in touch with you if something happens and I don't like the idea of you talking about things related to the *bedroom* with other people', he said, with a finality I greatly disliked.

'I didn't talk …', I start. 'I don't care', he said, interrupting my sentence before I could even begin.

I sat back against the bed, unsure how I ended up in a position where I was having to defend going out and doing my research. I hated being at home anyhow; he wouldn't let my family and friends come to visit anymore, so going out into the field was really the only way I could socialize apart from going into the office. 'I've said my piece, do what you want', he said, turning the lamp off and rolling away from me.

Two weeks later, I am standing in the bathroom packing up my toiletries for my flight, and he comes in. 'What are you doing?' he asks. 'I'm getting ready for my flight tomorrow', I say with as little emotion as I can. One of his favourite ways to torture me is to needle me until I break down, too upset to have a coherent conversation and he then acts all patient and understanding as if he is all rational and I am an emotional, hysterical child.

I refused to give him the satisfaction of upsetting me. I had made my decision to continue my fieldwork, which meant going against his wishes. Had he been a more reasonable person, I might have been able to meet him on some sort of middle ground. But over the years, he had slipped more and more towards being a sort of mini-dictator, unilaterally deciding for everyone in the house (i.e. me and the two cats) what we were doing.

I was finally done. I had reached my breaking point. I would not sacrifice almost ten years of study and hard work to make him happy. I had fought against myself for so long, wanting to be both the Good Girlfriend and the Witchy Anthropologist. I realized that the two couldn't coexist in this relationship and I had to make a choice.

'So you're going on your little holiday then', he sneered, belittling my fieldwork by refusing to use its actual name. 'I am', I said simply, enjoying the look of shock on his face. Taking a step forward, he was now standing over me, always his last resort – physical intimidation: 'I won't be here if you go on this trip', he said with a quiet menace. 'That works for me', I say with confidence, and, zipping up my toiletry bag, I walk out, leaving him alone in the bathroom.

God's police and damned witches

It's evening and I've arrived up north for my next round of fieldwork and interviews. I've been invited for dinner and drinks with Tiff and her housemates. Their shared house is warm and inviting, especially against the crisp autumn winds outside. After dinner, Tiff and I retire to her bedroom, which she shares with her husband. Nestling into the loveseat carved into a large window in her bedroom, Tiff grabs a pile of fuzzy blankets to wrap around our knees to stave off the chilly air creeping around our feet.

Tiff recalled walking back to her cabin at witchcamp, pausing to listen to the sounds of pleasure spiralling through the air towards her. The noises beckoned and scared her in equal measure. Over steamy cups of chamomile tea, she tells me that she would later discover that what she was hearing was a very intimate and hands-on workshop with 'a circle of people masturbating together'.

Tiff was raised in a hippie fundamentalist Christian family in Byron Bay, essentially the 'California' of Australia. Her mother and father grew their own food, which meant that, during her youth, Tiff was denied the pleasure of a McDonald's burger and fries. Speaking of denying pleasure: 'I came from a conservative background', she said, 'so my sex education was – *don't have it*'.

Abstinence-based sex education teaches students that sex outside marriage is immoral, sinful. While sexual health, or 'sex-ed', is taught across the board, the interpretation and level of detail taught are often left up to the schools. Growing up in the 1990s, Tiff and I had both attended conservative Christian schools and churches. Sex was treated just like the McDonald's burger, as something dirty that, if ingested, would pollute the body. Abstaining from sex until marriage was the only way to keep the body pure. This rule went double for girls.

In 1975 Anne Summers published her incredibly influential and provocative book *Damned Whores and God's Police*. The settler colonial project, she argued, led to the creation of a patriarchal gender order that reduced nineteenth-century women to one of two narrow roles: virtuous wives and mothers, dubbed 'God's police', and the transgressive 'damned whores'. These stereotypes have deep religious roots and a specific aim; to keep women in check. We can either aspire to be one of God's police or be branded as a damned whore.

In the context of this binary situation, sex is critical. Virtuous wives are restricted to participating in sex within the social contract and container of marriage, where it is performed as a type of labour. The purpose of this is twofold: to bring pleasure to her husband and for reproduction. Damned whores, on the other hand: well, their label spells out their relationship with sex. Sex both defines and damns them. The damned whore is an explicitly sexual category. Included in this category, Summers argues, are any women who are sexually 'liberated'.

The logics underlying the stereotypes of the God's police and the damned whores have far-reaching influences and implications. Sex education is one such arena. So where exactly do girls find out about sex if not at school or home? For young women like Tiff and me, most sex education came from teen girl magazines and conversations with our friends. Sitting in our bedrooms, we would pore over the 'sealed sections' of teen girl magazines, giggling and taking turns to make sure our parents weren't going to barge in on us and ask awkward questions. These stolen moments during sleepovers were certainly informative; together, we patched together some semblance of what it would mean to grow up, to get boobs, and *gasp* have sex. Remember this was in the days before the internet and Google.

The problem was that, every time I looked at the magazines and their nude diagrams, I was just as interested in looking at the pictures of the women at the different stages of 'breast' development. But because all my friends during high school were straight – or at least no one ever outwardly talked about being anything other than hetero – I kept these feelings to myself. I folded them up and kept them safely tucked in between the pages of my little purple glittery diary. I hoped that one day, after school, I would find people who not only understood these feelings, but who might even love me because of them.

Bedknobs and broomsticks

My bedroom was the place where I hid my diary, copies of those magazines and their forbidden sealed sections, and my earliest witchy artefacts. Like many teenage girls, my bedroom was a sacred space, a sanctuary from the outside world. In an essay first published in 1970, Angela McRobbie and Jenny Garber (2006) introduced the idea of 'bedroom culture' as a response to the absence of teenage girls from the analysis of subcultures at the time. They observed that, while boys could roam around the streets, carving out spaces to perform their subcultural rituals and identities, teenage girls were encouraged to spend their free time in their rooms, protected from danger and sexual impropriety. Thus the bedroom became the centre of the teen girls' world, reading magazines, listening to music and expressing themselves.

The devaluation of girls, especially their activities and lifestyles, is prevalent in popular culture, often portrayed as frivolous and vapid. Since McRobbie and Garber's essay was first published, the internet has transformed bedroom culture, first with sites like tumblr and then Instagram. Unsurprisingly, this trend has spread across to TikTok, with bedrooms serving as both the backdrops and the subject of their videos. Scrolling on TikTok, I often come across videos of witchy bedroom aesthetics, ranging in styles from #cottagecore to #whimsigoth.

I enjoy these videos mostly because they remind me so much of my favourite witchy movie of all time, *The Craft*. Released in 1996, it is often cited in papers on the rise of witchcraft among young teen girls in the 1990s, alongside other classics like *Practical Magic* and the series *Buffy the Vampire Slayer* and *Charmed*.

The Craft represents the pinnacle of witchy bedroom culture. In the film, four teenage girls – Nancy, Bonnie,

Rochelle and Sarah – bond over their shared misfit high-school status and their desire to experiment with witchcraft. In the opening scene, three of the four girls chant 'Now is the time, this is the hour, ours is the magic, ours is the power', which really captures the metaphor of magic and witchcraft in the film, the powerless seeking some form of power. Once the trio find their fourth member to complete the circle – Sarah – their magic begins to blossom and be used for a variety of reasons: to make a racist girl's hair fall out, to cause an abusive step-father to have a heart attack, to heal scars and to make a fuckboy fall obsessively in love. In short, their magic is a metaphor for the teen girls to find power.

Like Tiff, I was also raised in a Catholic community and school, so the conversations we had during the Reclaiming workshop were entirely foreign territory for both of us. Even the idea of talking about sex outside the bedroom, outside the context of a heteronormative relationship, was pretty earth-shattering. 'I really like that it's so open. Sex is normal, you know? people want to do it. So here is how to do it safely. Here is a set of communication tools about how to be very clear about what you do and don't want and how to keep yourself safe and also to enjoy yourself.' Staring out the window, Tiff reflected: 'But that way of thinking is so different from how we operate in society, it was a bit jarring.'

She's not wrong: the Western world has a long and complicated relationship with sex and pleasure. Christianity in particular has played a pivotal role in shaping how we think about and frame sex. For example, within a Christian cosmology, the relationship between the body and soul means they are not only separate from one another; the two exist in a state of constant conflict with one another. The body is framed as beastly, animal-like – something to be controlled and transcended. The desires of the animal-like human body must be denied in the pursuit of spiritual purity. If sexual desire and pleasure represent the polluting potential of the body, then shame and sin are the religious and social mechanisms of controlling this potentiality.

Saving women from their sexual nature

Anthropologists have written for decades about the idea that sexuality is something to be ashamed of, to be controlled. Turning to religion was an opportunity to 'transcend' our base nature and desires. These values dominated during the eighteenth and nineteenth centuries, particularly in the West. Sex was framed as something to be stripped of all enjoyment and freedom and creativity, to be performed only between men and women (married of course) and for the purpose of procreation.

Many of the colonizing efforts during the early periods of the empire were directed towards the oriental 'Other', the so-called uncivilized savages. Both women and other racial groups (i.e. non-Europeans) were classified as closer to this animal nature than men and therefore in greater need of sexual repression. Black women in particular have been compared to animals when it comes to their sexuality. This is often referred to as the Jezebel myth (Boulware et al. 2024), the stereotype that African women are hypersexual and immoral, which emerged during slavery as a rationalization for sexual relations between white men and Black women, especially sexual unions involving slavers and the enslaved.

The Church also played a significant role in enforcing and indoctrinating this idea that women had less control over their desires, and that control was therefore something that needed to be projected onto them (and their bodies). Starhawk writes:

> Misogyny became a strong element in mediaeval Christianity. Women, who menstruate and give birth, were identified with sexuality and therefore with evil. In the Church's view, women's

permeable and leaky bodies makes them more susceptible than men to the Devil's influence. *All witchcraft stems from carnal lust, which is in women insatiable,* stated in the *Malleus Maleficarum*. (In Mackay and Institoris 2009)

The *Malleus Maleficarum*, the most well-known treatise on witch-hunting, includes a section called 'How Witches Impede and Prevent the Power of Procreation', an anxiety that manifests itself in the figure of the menopausal witch who can no longer bear children *and* the child-free hypersexual witch. As Jessie Kindig (2018) writes, both of these versions of the witch represent mistrust of 'women not reproducing within the sanctioned family structure, or not reproducing at all'. This is why so many representations of the witch in pop culture, especially those present in the horror genre, depict the witch as a devourer of children. Either eating her own or by stealing others' children. The witch is the embodiment of society's worst fears and anxieties about what would happen if women lost control of their bodies and sexuality. That they would descend into a lustful and bestial state. In short, they must be 'saved' from their very own nature.

This 'saving' is most famously captured in our collective imagination by the waves of witch hunts in the fifteenth and sixteenth centuries that washed over Europe and to a lesser extent in America. In *Caliban and the Witch*, Marxist feminist scholar Silvia Federici (2004) argues that the witch-hunting panic that swept through early modern Europe from the fifteenth to the seventeenth century was motivated by the desire to claim women's reproductive capacity and sexuality for the state and for capital. Simply put, women needed to produce new workers in order for capitalism to function. An overt example of this can be seen in the early American policy that referred to enslaved women of childbearing age as 'increase' by slave owners because of their potential to add to their owner's wealth.

Federici argues that the control and regulation of women's bodies was part of the process Marx calls 'primitive accumulation'. The process of primitive accumulation involves gathering the raw material of labour and land on which modern industry and nation-states could be created. The control of women's reproduction was an important element of the enclosure of European common lands into private property.

During this period the nuclear family became the dominant framework for controlling women's reproduction. According to the Church, families are meant to reflect the holy hierarchy that places men at the head of the household. A Marxist feminist would say that it is the exploitative relations of capitalism that cause exploitative patriarchal relations within the family. What this means is that, while individual men may benefit from the unpaid domestic labour and childcare largely undertaken by women, it is the capitalist system that is the main cause of women being in the subordinate role of the housewife. Contemporary witchcraft is a movement that resists this co-option and control over women's reproductive labour. Since it does not exist outside of capitalist or colonial systems, it is not immune to the ideologies and techniques of these very systems.

The Church of Wicca

The idea – or more accurately the *ideal* – of the nuclear family became intrinsic to how the Church and early stages of capitalism exerted control over women's bodies, specifically in terms of reproduction. This became apparent for Temperance, whom I met for lunch one day during my fieldwork trip to Queensland.

'It's hard when you already know the answers they're going to give you to your questions about sex. It's totally scripted. You want something deeper and meaningful and all they spit back at you is what the Bible says. I was sick of that. I don't think I ever had faith in God, but the people; I had faith in them. But they suppressed their sexuality and it came out in the worst ways like people having affairs. It all crashed around me when I was fifteen. That's when I walked away from it all. Religion. Spirituality. All of it.' This is what Temperance, now twenty-five, tells me over soymilk lattes at an outdoor café in Queensland.

You don't get baptized until you're at least fifteen, she explains to me. Unlike other Christian denominations like Catholicism, which baptizes infants, in Temperance's family's local church, members make the conscious choice to join the congregation when they turn fifteen. Her decision to leave the Church was not simple or straightforward. Leaving also meant turning away from her entire family's belief system, especially with her dad's history as a missionary and a Church pastor. It wasn't until she started university and met Tiff that they both began exploring what they called 'alternate new agey wishy washy sort of stuff with crystals'. During this period of exploration and 'dabbling', Temperance realized she wasn't 'really feeling any of it'; what she actually needed was 'something deeper and wanted a community'. While she didn't miss the hypocrisy or the sexual suppression of her Church, she did miss 'having somewhere you can go to talk to someone about spirituality'. Stirring her coffee thoughtfully, she added: 'I miss having a network of people who may not be on the same path as you but understand that you're on a path.'

The way Temperance was feeling mirrored so many of the other people I had encountered. These largely white, middle-class and educated folks feel that working hard under capitalism, ascribing to the Protestant work ethic, has failed to live up to its promises. They find themselves feeling empty and disconnected. And so they turn to a wild and syncretic, no holds barred form of contemporary spirituality to attempt to fill that void. In her search for community and a sense of belonging, Temperance came across Wicca, which she found was almost the witchy equivalent of her childhood Church. 'It was so scripted', she said, wrinkling her nose at the memory; 'they had the *sacred bowl* and the *sacred paper*. It just seemed a bit wanky to be honest. They almost felt desperate to call what they were doing a religion.' I could tell that Wicca rubbed Temperance in all the wrong ways.

Wicca gained a lot of traction in the 1990s, not just amongst practitioners but in the public eye. I was certainly part of the wave of teen girls who couldn't get enough of wonder-women like Prue, Piper, Phoebe and Paige from *Charmed* and Willow and Tara from *Buffy the Vampire Slayer*. While the familiar trope of the spooky witch in the woods didn't fully dissipate, this decade opened the doors for a whole spectrum of different witch manifestations. From wholesome homemaker, to gothy outsider, or sexy seductress – this decade showed that witches don't have a singular look, motivation or personality.

While Wicca may have become more fashionable during the 1990s, it actually dates back much further than that. As a movement, most historians trace the genesis of witchcraft as *movement* back to one scraggly and eccentric old Englishman: Gerald Gardner, godfather of Wicca. Gardner established many of the core aspects of Wicca and witchcraft that we recognize today. Initiation into witchcraft is often portrayed in popular culture as both grotesque and titillating. A major part of the mythology and lore surrounding Gardner is the story that he was initiated into a coven of witches that supposedly survived the witch hunts of the sixteenth and seventeenth centuries, predating Christianity and practising in secret for fear of persecution. According to Gardner, one cold autumnal night in 1939, he was taken by the coven to a large house owned by a wealthy local woman, where he was made to strip naked and taken through an initiation ceremony. The legacy of initiation in Wicca has been heavily shaped by this supposed encounter with a surviving coven and by Gardner's own writing on the subject:

> And it is for this reason that a man may only be taught by a woman and a woman by a man, and that man and man, and woman and woman, should never attempt these practices together. And may all the Curses of the Mighty Ones be on any who make the attempt. (1961: 32)

Gardner reasons that learning the craft often leads to feelings of 'fondness' to develop between teachers and students, which can be pursued if they wish. However, to prevent this relationship forming between same-sex pairings, Gardner advises that only men teach women, and vice versa. For those who follow Gardner's teachings, often called Wiccans, the symbolic efficacy of the magical ritual stems from the result of the symbolic union of male and female polarities. This belief slides down the slippery slope of essentializing gender with biological sex.

This tendency to equate female with women and male with men 'rubbed' Temperance 'the wrong way'. Picking the burnt cheese off her toasted sandwich she explained: 'There are traditions where you have to be initiated by someone of the opposite sex, for me that's just really weird.' Admiring her handiwork, she took a bite and after chewing thoughtfully for a few moments she added: 'In a lot of those same traditions, the initiation has to be a sexual exchange and it can be symbolic *but* not always.'

The symbolic version of this sexual exchange that Temperance was referring to is called the Great Rite, a fertility ritual where the High Priest, representative of the God, dipping the ceremonial dagger called the athame into the cup held by the High Priestess, is meant to symbolize the (pro)creative union of both deities. 'Even if it is symbolic and you are just putting an athame in a cup, that still doesn't sit right with me.'

To borrow Temperance's language, the next step on her 'path' was Reclaiming Witchcraft and her first encounter with the broader Reclaiming community was through the WitchCamp.

'So how was your experience at the sacred kink workshop?' I asked.

'It was interesting, I really appreciated that they held it. It was an important conversation to have', she said. 'I've been with my partner seven years and after that much time you start to explore and you trust each other more. I wouldn't consider myself a kink on the spectrum of things but things have started to come up. Like why do I feel shame, why is that my reaction to certain things?'

'I completely understand', I say. I pause, thinking about whether I want to share something with her. *Well she's opening up to me about her sex life, only fair I reciprocate.* 'I um, wanted to try some things after the workshop, and my partner – *ex-partner, I say in my head, although I'm not quite ready to come to terms with that just yet* – but I didn't know how to ask for that, or if I should even want to do that in the first place.'

'Exactly!' Temperance said. 'It's the gender thing, I am an avid feminist and surrendering feels threatening. Surrendering to a man feels extremely difficult. I will get halfway then all of a sudden go *oooh shit*. Even though I know he's not forcing me to do anything, like I'm the one initiating it. It's just weird. Like, is it a deep-seated misogyny that's in me? Like, am I asking for this kind of thing because it's a way that society has trained my brain?'

This societal 'training' as Temperance puts it, also called socialization, is exactly what Anne Summers was criticizing in her book. The ways our culture and social norms, religious beliefs and rituals all work together to support the idea that women have very few pathways in life. The virtuous wife, 'God's police', or the transgressors, the so-called 'damned whores'. The Good Girlfriend or the Witch.

I didn't realize it, but my decision to continue my fieldwork, which I knew meant the end of my relationship, a six-year relationship, would lead me down a new and uncharted path. One where I would meet fairies, witches and even a Voodoo priestess or two, many women who had stepped outside what society considered to be 'good' and 'normal' and 'appropriate' for them. Most importantly, I began to meet myself, and undergo the unpleasant but necessary process of unpacking the beliefs about myself that I had been conditioned to accept.

4

The Nature Witch

'What kind of dog did you get?'

Fae's green eyes twinkle in the late morning sun, her feet folded up under her as she leans against the wooden balcony table. She's inquisitively peering over at the china pattern on my teacup that the hippie/hipster barista has placed in front of me. Steam rolls off the cup as I breathe in the clove, cinnamon and cardamom pods steeping in the hot water, slowly releasing their delicious warmth. 'I think it's a Lassie dog', I say, picking up a teaspoon of warm honey, watching the glob slowly spiral and fall into the tea. The honey warms mid-air with the heat of the tea and sunshine, thinning into a spiderweb-thin strand. I wiggle my spoon and watch with childish joy as the strand creates a little tapestry on top of my tea. The honey sits atop the almond milk for a few moments before it drops to the bottom of the teacup and I have a few seconds to enjoy the little woven pattern I've made for myself. Finally plopping my spoon into the tea and stirring the honey, chai and almond milk together, I return the question to Fae: 'What kind of dog did you get?'

This café was the kind of place that had mismatched chairs, cutlery and cups that made it seem effortlessly cool and whimsical without trying too hard. Somehow, we both ended up with teacups decorated with English garden flowers like roses and chrysanthemums, and, for some strange reason, different dog breeds. 'I got a Dobermann', she said with a snort. 'Do you think they're trying to tell me something?'

Her joke reminded me of something a witch had told me a few months ago. 'How do you know if someone is a witch?' I asked her. She slowly leant forward, looking me dead in the eyes, and said slowly: 'It's something you feel deep in your gut. Not in your head, not in your mind – we're like dogs. We can just sense one another.'

So, do you ever go to the CloudCatcher witchcamps? I asked Fae. 'Nah', she said, 'that's not really my jam. I think those events are great for activists and such, especially if they're burnt out. My coven is in Tassie [Tasmania] and what we do is a different kind of craft.' What kind is that? I ask. 'Well, what we do is closer to the Robert Cochrane tradition', she said.

Robert Cochrane is one of the lesser-known figures of the contemporary British witchcraft movement and founder of The Clan of Tubal Cain. Born into a working-class family, Cochrane would later claim that members of his own family had been practitioners of an ancient pagan witch-cult since at least the seventeenth century, and that two of them had been executed for it (White 2018). Like Gardner, claiming familial connections to an ancient pagan witch-cult brought a sentence of legitimacy and legacy to their covens. In this context, the claim of 'ancientness' is also invoked as an act of resistance. By linking ancient religions and their contemporary practice, groups like Cochrane's highlight the possibility that 'patriarchy and god-worship are not normative and that "goddess" can be a useful symbol for women today' (Rountree 2003: 4).

Cochrane had told the members of his coven that his great-grandfather was one of the last Grand Masters of the Staffordshire witches and that his grandparents had abandoned the craft and converted to Methodism to protect themselves. He claimed that his father had practised witchcraft, but that he kept it a secret and, after his father's death, was taught the ways of the craft by his mother and his aunt. The witches of the Clan of Tubal Cain revere a Horned God and Fate, who often take the form of the ancient Greek goddess Hekate. According to Cochrane, the goddess of witches was a weaver and therefore the tools for weaving and spinning became symbols for the threads of fate that permeate, bind and, ultimately, order the universe (Howard 2011).

'So how does magic work in the Cochrane tradition?', I ask Fae, sipping on my chai. Frowning in concentration, she replied, as she twirled the spoon in her coffee: 'It's the way I believe, that just stirring my coffee may or may not affect an old mate across the town. But, if I had his hair and I was stirring that into something, maybe it would, you know what I mean? We're all connected to each other, threads of fate all interwoven together into a web. We are all connected, which is why sorcery works, y'know? Having those links makes it more powerful.'

In this strange and delightful microcosm, Fae whispered to me the questions that had dogged me since I first set out on this journey. How does one become a witch? Is it like the Catholicism I was so familiar with and accustomed to? A tradition with clear rites and rituals for initiation such as baptism and confirmation with all the trappings and celebration? Or is it something deeper, darker and more layered? Were the tiny everyday rituals and moments just as important as the larger and louder productions?

Weaving magic

Hair is a powerful cultural object, a material used in rituals and ceremonies across the world. In Hinduism, babies on their first birthday undergo the *mundan*, a hair-shaving ceremony. The rite of passage is believed to purify the baby of any negativity from their past life, while promoting mental and spiritual development. In Voodoo rituals, hair is often incorporated into the creation of ritual artefacts, with Voodoo dolls being one of the most famous examples of this practice.

The type of ritual Fae described to me is closer to creating a Voodoo doll, because it uses something from another person's body (such as hair) to effect some kind of change, which relies on the idea of contagious magic. Through contagious magic, people can be influenced through the transfer of their essence via objects, like hair or nail clippings, saliva or even blood. These objects are treated as symbolically equal to the person from whose body they came, meaning that whatever you do to one body will have the same effect on the other. This type of magical belief is tethered to the idea that there is a material and an immaterial connection between a person and body parts that have been separated from an individual.

Finishing our chai, Fae and I decide to move our conversation to the grassy hill next to the café. Behind the small set of shops was a stretch of trees which provided the perfect setting for our spontaneous ritual. Sitting behind Fae, I take a small section of hair right at the nape of her neck, and gently begin weaving the strands together into a simple plait. 'So where did this idea come from?', I ask her. She was the one who suggested we weave some blessings into each other's hair. 'Well it reminds me of an old sailor's tale my mum would tell me, about how women would weave wishes into their hair so that their men would come home safe. They would gift them woven pieces of thread to undo only when they want to release the wind.'

'So we're weaving wishes into each other's hair, that will eventually unravel and let the wishes out?' I ask.

'That's right', she says.

'In that case', I say, 'what would you like me to weave into your plait?'

'What would I like? Well there is a particular flavour of longing and lack that's been dogging me lately and I reckon I'm ready to let that dissipate.' I gently take the small section of hair Fae offered me and begin to plait it. 'Where do you feel it?', I ask.

Patting her chest, she tells me: 'It's there. You know I think that's going to block blessings that could be coming so I'm ready for blessings. I welcome them and, yeah, let it ease. I want to let that ease so I feel like I'm enough.'

While she spoke, my fingers pull and loop her long silky red hair together, and part of me feels a twinge of jealousy. An old jealousy, the same one that made me jealous of my friends in high school and their long, shiny blonde hair. As I come to the end of the plait, I realize out loud: 'I don't have any hair bands with me to secure it.' She says: 'That's better, it will unravel instead of being ripped out.'

I stood up, brushing some of the grass and dirt that had collected on my jeans and repositioned myself in front of Fae in anticipation of my own plait. Closing my eyes I could feel the dappled sunlight on my cheeks, I could smell the earthy scent of the ground beneath us and hear the lorikeets high in the tree singing to each other.

'What would you like me to weave into your plait?', she asks, as her hands worked their way through my hair, finding a section of my curls to plait. I felt my voice catch in my throat and a tightness spread across my chest. I hadn't told anyone about my break-up and speaking it aloud felt like I was making it real. I had spent most of my twenties with him, we had basically grown up together. A prickle of shame crept across my mind as I realized in that moment that the real reason I was so scared to leave him, no matter how badly he treated me, was that being miserable was better than being alone.

How was I supposed to ask for what I really wanted, to admit that what I wanted her to weave into my plait was for me to feel safe and happy and worthy of feeling loved. 'I, uh', I say, my voice shaking, 'I need strength.' I could feel Fae pause and consider her words carefully as she asks slowly and tactfully: 'What do you need the strength for, if you don't mind me asking?' Sucking in the humid air, I manage to squeak out: 'The strength to be alone, and be okay with that.' I feel Fae smile behind me as she interweaves her fingers through my hair. She had given me the gift of the space I needed to say something aloud I couldn't admit to my loved ones just yet. There really are some things you can only tell a stranger.

The weaving ritual we performed rested on a curious interplay between seemingly incongruous beliefs. The belief in fate or determinism, the idea that all events, including human action, are ultimately determined by causes that are external to the will. And the belief in agency, a sentiment captured perfectly by the Wiccan Rede, 'an' ye harm none, do what ye will'. I asked myself, how could it be that witches, like Fae, believe in both of these things at the same time?

All her talk about webs and weaving threads of fate reminded me of a story anthropologist Tim Ingold (2008) tells about a conversation between an ant and a spider. In his tale, Spider strikes up a conversation with Ant about what it's like to live in a colony. As a solitary creature, she is curious about what it is like to be social. They talk to one another on the floor of the forest surrounded by what Ant (the network builder) sees as a collection of distinct objects and what Spider (the web weaver) sees as a mesh of interlaced threads. What this means is that Ant acts as an individual within his colony (aka society), whereas Spider is an individual acting through a range of interrelated connections within its web.

This story helps me understand how Fae sees the world, which is closer to the spider than the ant. She recognizes that agency isn't a process that happens between actors (ant to ant); rather, it is something that is deeply interwoven with the environment and the material world. The natural world is not something that actors (ants) exist within and act upon; instead, through the eyes of the spider, the world is made up of a meshwork of relationships between living and non-living. Life, social life, is not something the person *does*, but what the person *undergoes*: a process in which human beings both grow and are grown, developing and maturing – from birth through infancy and childhood into adulthood and old age – within a web of relationships established through the presence and activities of others.

This is what I believe Fae means when she says she believes in fate. She explains to me that when it comes to developing and embracing change, 'many people are scared to take that leap of faith.'

'What do you mean if people are scared? Scared of what?' I ask.

'They're scared to lose parts of themselves', she says, leaning back onto the grassy hill. 'If they've spent all this time building up ideas about themselves, they start to calcify. If they leap and they fall, then they're meant to. You have to smash it down yourself and have some midlife crisis.'

The idea of the midlife crisis usually conjures up images of a forty-something-year-old man who, realizing he is halfway through his life, begins to struggle with his identity and, to make up for his newfound insecurity, buys a shiny red car and starts dating someone much, much younger than himself. Now usually when this trope turns up in Hollywood, it's for a laugh, but what it does is highlight an important part of social life that involves transitions, rites of passage that mark the movement from one life stage to another. Which is why I ask Fae: 'Is initiation important in your tradition?' Looking at me thoughtfully, she replies: 'Yes, but I don't think you do it once. It's a process of harrowing you know.'

Harrowing seemed to me to be an unusual word to use when talking about initiations. The *Oxford English Dictionary* defines harrowing as a verb that means to 'tear, lacerate, wound'. Which makes more sense, considering how Fae defines an initiation or rite of passage as the smashing of pieces of one's identity. Most people understandably avoid these types of rituals. I mean, who wouldn't? They don't exactly sound like sunshine and rainbows.

Beware fairy circles

The 'harrowing' part of these types of processes, I believe, stems from how close they play into the realm of the liminal. It is the fear of the unknown, of uncertainty, that dogs this particular definition of a rite of passage. Liminal is a word that gets tossed around quite a lot and is used often as a synonym for 'betweenness', which isn't too far off. Every morning, I think about liminal spaces as I pass by a ring of mushrooms that forms on the dewy grass outside my house. By the evening, they disintegrate and fall back to the earth, but in the morning, they sit upright, pale white in the sunlight. These circles are commonly known in European folklore as fairy circles, and are one of my favourite examples of a 'liminal space'. As the stories go, they are gateways to the fairy realm and if one steps into the circle, one risks being kidnapped (or blessed, depending on the myth and region) by fairies. Now I don't believe in the fairy realm per se, but I make a point to not step into these circles, nonetheless.

This is just a small example of a liminal space, but liminality extends to people and time. Midnight is featured heavily in horror movies not only because it's late at night, but because it represents the transitory and spooky period between night and day. You have probably heard the adage before that on Halloween the veil that separates the living and the dead is at its thinnest, which is where many of the customs we associate with the day come from. For instance, carving pumpkins and lighting a candle was initially intended to ward off evil spirits.

Liminal, in an anthropological sense, means 'without status'. That which is 'in between' is neither one thing nor the other and is, therefore, dangerous. In a witchy context, where things that are dangerous like taboos are purposefully played with, liminality becomes the ultimate magical dirt.

When it comes to people undergoing rites of passage, anthropologist Victor Turner's theory (1969) sets out three key stages: separation, the liminal period and reincorporation. Put simply, the first stage is when the individual moves away from their position in their social group. They then move into the liminal period where they are neither in their original position nor have they moved through the threshold into their new one. Finally, once they move past the threshold of the liminal, they become reincorporated into their community.

A simple example of this process can be observed in school children. When they move from primary school to high school, they transition from childhood into being a teenager. Then, when they graduate from high school, they move into adulthood. Different cultures and religions have their own rituals for marking these rites of passage. Witches have their own types of rituals they use for marking transitions. These rituals deliberately set out to create liminal spaces.

Anthropologist Lynne Hume argues that witchcraft rituals draw on a range of sensory and embodied techniques to create a liminal space in order to facilitate transformative experiences where 'reality is momentarily suspended':

> Communication is not limited to mere words. An entire sensory repertoire is used to convey dramatic messages:

> breathing, dance movements, body posture and decoration, masks and paint, olfactory stimulation, the use of light and shadow, the mystery of foreign words, tone inflection, and even silence, all of which are fully employed to heighten activity and emotional response. In play, there is a freedom from normative constraints; one steps out of one time into another and enters an enclave within which it seems anything may happen. (1997: 7)

At the witchcamp I attended, I experienced many different types of rituals, from ones that involved the whole camp to smaller more intimate rituals that included just a handful of people. For the most part, my experience of those rituals was as an anthropologist. I would be participating, but at the same time thinking about what different props or procedures or gestures meant. It wasn't until the third night of camp that a ritual was finally held outside because the rain had let up. Our small group had been chosen to open the ritual, to invite the elements and deities to join us. I was a little jittery, nervous about performing in front of the whole camp. As night fell, I haunted the edge of the grassy hill, watching people build and tend the bonfire we would encircle.

At all the rituals, I had been wearing my own clothes, everyday shirts and jeans, unlike experienced campers who would don ritual wear when it was time to enter ritual space. This time, I borrowed a friend's dress and picked out a matching purple mask from the collective costume table. Some were painting each other's faces, others finding feathers to braid into their hair.

The new clothes and mask I was wearing, together with the smell of the smoke rising from the fire and the deep chanting voices reverberating around the circle, changed me. Before I stepped into the circle, I was Emma the anthropologist, there to do fieldwork and collect data to write up and interpret later. Once I stepped into the circle I underwent a change, one that was not perceptible to the naked eye but significant nonetheless. In the liminal space of the ritual I became Emma the witch.

A war on witches

Something I love about being around witches is their talent as storytellers. The more time I spent around them, visiting them, having cups of tea at their houses and going for walks together, the more I noticed one particular story being told. The details varied from family to family, woman to woman, and were inflected by their own cultural background; the essence, however, remained the same.

The story goes that once upon a time, before Christianity spread across continents, there were no large institutional religions; instead, people practised their own regional folk-based traditions. When these larger 'world' religions began to take over territories alongside the larger colonial project, they were not simply pushed aside. They were actively vilified and their proponents persecuted. However, these traditions and beliefs managed to survive, protected until it was safe enough to practise them out in the open.

If this sounds familiar, it should do. It's the same story Gerald Gardner told to his followers and Robert Cochrane recounted his own version to his own coven. Starhawk has also told her own version of the story of the destruction of this 'matriarchal utopia' that existed in pre-Christian Celtic communities:

> Communications between covens were severed; no longer could they meet on the Great Festivals to share knowledge and exchange the results of spells or rituals. Parts of the tradition became lost or forgotten. Yet somehow, in secret, in silence, over glowing coals, behind closed shutters, encoded as fairy

tales and folk songs, or hidden in subconscious memories, the seed was passed on. (1979: 20)

One young witch I spent time with – Morgan – adored the folk songs by one popular pagan artist called Damh the Bard. His songs were used for a short film called *The Spirit of Albion*, which Morgan showed me one afternoon. We curled up on her family's lounge with her cat and her best friend and fellow D&D player to watch the movie. The film had a student-like quality that was a little cringey, but what I found most interesting was watching Morgan's reactions to certain parts of the film, and when she loudly and excitedly explained different parts of the movie: 'There's Morrighan and that's Ceridwen and oooh that's Pan.'

In the film, each of these ancient Celtic gods makes contact with a person living in the twenty-first century, who in their own way is lost or unhappy in their lives. They go on a journey together and discover that, to reconnect with themselves and with nature and to find meaning in life, they need to remember the old gods and the traditions of their pre-Christian ancestors. These stories have a shiny, utopian quality to them. This is in large part because witches such as Gerald Gardner, Robert Cochrane and Starhawk were all influenced by archaeologist and folklorist Margaret Murray.

Margaret Alice Murray was born into a wealthy family in Calcutta while India was still under British rule (Sheppard 2013). She grew up travelling between India and England, and spent her young life exploring the Mediterranean, the Middle East and Europe. She began studying Egyptology at University College London in 1894 and later taught there; she was the first woman to be appointed as a lecturer in archaeology in the United Kingdom. A single woman in the academy, and a feminist activist and suffragist, she continually fought on behalf of the women coming to study at university.

Most of her early written work was on Egyptology, and she worked to bring the subject into the public realm. Unable to return to Egypt due to the First World War, she focused her research on the witch-cult hypothesis, the theory that the witch trials of Early Modern Christendom were an attempt to extinguish a surviving pre-Christian, pagan religion devoted to a Horned God. She began writing papers on the subject before fully articulating her views in her 1921 book *The Witch-Cult in Western Europe*. After the book was published, it received criticism for distorting and misrepresenting the sources she was drawing upon. She argued that before Christianity swept through Europe there existed an ancient religion, one where women could hold positions of religious authority and rituals designed around fertility and Celtic mythologies. Over time, as Christianity grew in power, the Church waged war against this ancient religion and its adherents, articulated in the Papal Bull of Innocent VIII, which launched the inquisition into the 'malign presence of witches and witchcraft in the Holy Roman Empire' (Deyrmenjian 2020).

Murray's theory of Christianity's war against the ancient religion (also called Old Religion, the witch-cult, or the Dianic cult) and the survival of that religion into the modern age was incredibly popular. Most of the theories surrounding the witch hunts of mediaeval Europe focused on rationalist explanations, arguing that the people who were persecuted and executed were 'victims of superstition, ignorance, and hysterical panics whipped up by the Churches for devious political or financial reasons' (Noble 2005: 8). Both academics and the broader public were tired of this framing, eager for something more meaty and exciting.

Rather than framing those being accused as innocent victims caught up in the hysteria and moral panic of the time, Murray presented witches as real people and went into an intimate level of detail about their traditions and beliefs. She argues in her book that many of the rituals and beliefs were focused around fertility, which was then twisted and perverted by the Church into the myth that witches use their powers to cause crops to fail, livestock to die and miscarriages to take place. This idea ties directly into the image of a utopian past, where witches (also referred to as heathens and pagans) lived a simpler life. This idea was particularly appealing to the nineteenth-century Romantics reading her book, who were pushing back against Christianity as well as the pollution and social decay accompanying the birth of the Industrial Revolution.

Another influential development during this time was the rise of pseudo-archaeology, also called fringe or junk archaeology, which describes attempts to intercept archaeological subjects while ignoring the long established scientific methods of the discipline. For example, the recent rise of people believing that aliens built the pyramids. In a broader pagan context, pseudo-archaeology is manifest in the form of beliefs about things like the alleged historic association between Druidry and Stonehenge (Cusack 2012). Or the Goddess movement, which has been 'thoroughly critiqued by some feminists for mythologizing and misrepresenting the past to serve a contemporary socio-political and religious agenda' and 'for re-invoking unhelpful essentialist ideas about "woman as nature" and nurturer' (Rountree 2003: 5).

A cult of women

Murray's theory of a matriarchal prehistory became the bedrock for other popular pagan literature that emerged during the 1970s and '80s, such as Merlin Stone's *When God Was a Woman* (1976), where she makes the controversial argument that peaceful, benevolent matriarchal society and Goddess-reverent traditions were attacked, undermined and ultimately destroyed almost completely by the ancient tribes, including

Hebrews and early Christians. The claims made by authors such as Stone and others that rest on Murray's theory have been the subject of heated debates among feminist scholars. Cynthia Eller, for example, argues that inventing prehistoric ages in which women and men lived in harmony and equality – aka 'matriarchal myth' – leaves the feminist movement open to accusations of 'vacuousness and irrelevance that we cannot afford to court' (2000: 8).

Tied closely to Murray's theory of an ancient witch-cult organized around celebrating and nurturing fertility is the belief that women are naturally maternal and therefore have an innate connection to nature. Barbara Ehrenreich and Deirdre English connect the struggles facing second wave feminists in the medical sector with the women persecuted during the Church's war on witchcraft:

> The central idea was that the medical profession as we knew it (still over 90 percent male) had replaced and driven out a much older tradition of female lay healing, including both midwifery and a range of healing skills, while closing medical education to women. In other words, the ignorance and disempowerment of women that we confronted in the 1970s were not long standing conditions, but were the result of a prolonged power struggle that had taken place in America in the early nineteenth century, well before the rise of scientific medicine. We traced a similar power struggle in Europe back to the early modern era and we looked at how female lay healers of the same era were frequently targeted as 'witches'. (2010: 11)

Contemporary witchcraft practitioners have absorbed both Murray's theory and Ehrenreich and English's work, intertwining them to make sense of how (and why) the world and culture they live in devalues women and witches. They hold onto this idea that, through successive cycles of oppression, there has been a distinct cultural shift away from traditions of women-healers, women-shamans and women-leaders towards male dominance of these fields.

While Murray's theory has been thoroughly debated and 'debunked' in the academic world, her ideas have taken root within the wider witchy community and appear in various forms and iterations throughout most traditions. Some witches believe wholeheartedly in the idea that, before colonization and the Church's war on women, there was a utopian-like world, one where women held places of social and political power tied in part to their knowledge of particular crafts, with medicine and midwifery being the prime example that Ehrenreich and English focus on in their work.

There is certainly an appealing and almost romanticized quality to this tale, that once upon a time women weren't oppressed and nature was sacred. Then came the big three C's: colonialism and capitalism and Christianity fucked it all up. I'm not a fan of the big three at the best of times; however, the danger in this story is in its simplicity: it smooths over some of the complex and often brutal details of history with its broad brushstrokes. I would also argue that this story risks reducing women to their biological functions and erasing trans women entirely. Speculative fiction writer Ursula K. Le Guin put it quite eloquently in her book *Words Are My Matter*:

> But I didn't and still don't like making a cult of women's knowledge, preening ourselves on knowing things men don't know, women's deep irrational wisdom, women's instinctive knowledge of Nature, and so on. All that all too often merely reinforces the masculinist idea of women as primitive and inferior – women's knowledge as elementary, primitive, always down below at the dark roots, while men get to cultivate and own the flowers and crops that come up into the light. But why should women keep talking baby talk while men get to grow up? Why should women feel blindly while men get to think? (2016: 172)

Le Guin's hesitancy to form a cult around women's innate 'instinctive knowledge of Nature' runs in opposition to the core of the utopian story of the matriarchal prehistory, the story that grounds so many of the beliefs and rituals practised by witches today. I experienced this same reluctance as I was sitting in Willow's backyard, surrounded by the circle of women celebrating their womanly cycles. All their talk of *blood magic* and *sacred wombs* made me cringe internally, even though, at the time, I couldn't quite put my finger on why that was.

The source of my cringe was the biological essentialism underlying these beliefs. Biological essentialism is the conflation of sex and gender as one and the same, and the belief that gender differences are an intrinsic result of biology. This topic has a long history in contemporary witchcraft, with ongoing debates between witchcraft practitioners and feminist scholars (Daly 1978; Eller 2000) about the matriarchal prehistory myth and the resulting beliefs and rituals that essentialize a connection between woman, nature and nurturance (Ortner 1974).

A key point of contention in these debates centres around how the gender binary of male/female and god/goddess creates conflicts within witchy (and more broadly pagan) communities about the inclusion – and sometimes resulting exclusion – of transgender individuals. Christine Hoff Kraemer (2012: 390) highlights the paradoxical relationship the pagan community has with gender and sexuality, where, on the one hand, the community is perceived to be relatively 'accepting of same-sex relationships, BDSM, polyamory, transgender, and other expressions of gender and sexuality that are marginalized by mainstream society.' On the other hand, there are more politically conservative traditions and groups, where transgender individuals are excluded from single-gender groups and rituals.

The increase in gay, lesbian and transgender presence at events and festivals has been noted by a number of pagan and witchcraft scholars (Neitz 2000; Lepage 2017; Ezzy 2014). It was something I also observed at the CloudCatcher witchcamp, where attendees played with gender through language (male-presenting individuals calling themselves a priestess), and through dress (female-presenting individuals wearing horns, traditionally 'masculine' adornments). This playfulness and this openness to fluidity, which Lepage and I both observed in the Reclaiming tradition in Australia and Montreal, respectively, stem from queerness, which Yvonne Aburrow (2009: 156) defines as 'radically resistant to normativity'.

A now famous example of queer resistance occurred at the Pantheacon, described as the largest indoor gathering of Pagans in North America, which held its last annual conference in 2020. At the 2011 Pantheacon, there were a number of events, one of which was a devotional ritual held in honour of Lilith, a feminine figure theorized to be the first wife of Adam, rumoured to have been 'banished' from the Garden of Eden for not complying with and obeying him. Lilith's story of oppression is a favourite amongst the witchy and the Pagan; take, for example, Lady Haight-Ashton's (2019: 2) description of Lilith, which exemplifies the witchy interpretation of Lilith as a symbol of feminine resistance: 'Lilith, the first female, created equal to stand as a partner ... but she proved to be a person so troublesome that she vanishes from her rightful place in civilization's mythological legends in place of Eve, the first wife.'

During the 2011 Pantheacon a devotional ritual for Lilith was held that kicked off a series of debates and controversies both during and following the conference. The 'Rite of Lilith' was run by the Amazon Priestess Tribe (a group that exists within the umbrella group the *Come As You Are Coven*) and intended to include only genetic females, or 'female-born women' (according to the website). This detail was left out of the programme, which the 'event organizers stated was a regrettable oversight, which led to several transwomen and one male to be turned away from the ritual' (Kraemer 2010: 277). During the controversy, Sarah Thompson penned 'An open letter to all pagans, and particularly the Pantheacon organizers', in response to both the Lilith ritual controversy and other issues regarding gender and sexuality bubbling away at the Pantheacon for a number of years:

> It is my not so humble opinion that a lot of nonsense is talked about gender in magick. Some people say that women can (or should) only deal with female deity, and that men can only deal with male deity. Some, including many from other branches of my own tradition, say that only through the interplay of male and female energies can magick be enacted. Some claim that gay people can not perform magick. Some say that transsexual and transgendered people are similarly disconnected from the current. Personal experience, and that of many people I've worked with, illustrates that this simply isn't so. It's just so much superstitious nonsense. (2011: n.p.)

This letter was circulated at the 2011 Pantheacon and 'sparked intense discussion in many groups', thereby achieving one of their goals: to move the 'discussion about gender and transgender ... from grumblings to wide open conversation' (Thompson et al. 2012: ix). The events during and after the controversies at the 2011 Pantheacon are also detailed on the Open Source Alexandrian Witchcraft Tradition website (https://st4r.org/), in blog posts from individuals who were present (and turned away from the Lilith ritual), in the open letter and at the Crow Ritual (which ended up not being performed).

The Open Source Alexandrian Witchcraft Tradition website does an amazing job at archiving the events that took place.[10] Queer community archives are created by a desire to document

---

10   https://st4r.org/information-archive/.

histories that are not collected or recognized by mainstream archival institutions. In many ways, they are a form of archival activism. Here I call on Ann Cvetkovich's description of queer archives as many things, including 'magical collections of documents that represent far more than the literal value of the objects themselves' (2003: 268). Take, for example, the Open Source archive containing the Crow Ritual-that-never-was, which captures the feelings that arose during the events surrounding the 2011 Pantheacon:

> I, Crow, banish the assumption that just because we're pagans, that we don't have issues of gender, class, race, and other discrimination in our ranks!
> I challenge each of you: pagan, heathen, ceremonial magician, witch, lord, lady, fae, druid, young, old, queer, straight, cis-gendered, transgendered, male, female to look within yourselves, your groups, and this community and see that yes, you do this. Yes, you do harm, even if you don't realize it.
> I, Crow, charge each and every one of you to challenge the old ideas of gender and magick.[11]

The closing remarks from the Crow Ritual carry both the frustration and the hope for the future of the Pagan and witchy community.

Temples, tents and taboos

On one level I understand the desire to make these bodily processes sacred when historically they have been a subject of shame. I can still remember my confusion when my family travelled from Sydney and stopped to visit the local Hindu

---

11   https://st4r.org/crow-ritual-pantheacon-2011/.

temple. My mum gently stopped me before I started to take my shoes off, whispering: 'I'm sorry Em, you can't go in while you have your period.' Confused and a little upset about being left outside while the family ventured inside, I asked her on the car ride home: 'Mum, why can't I go into the temple?' She sighed heavily and said: 'It has to do with the blood, it's impure and if you're bleeding you can't go into the temple.'

Unsatisfied with her answer, I decided to do my own research as a curious and somewhat precocious teenager who was more than a bit miffed at being left out. Growing up away from Fiji and away from any members of my family (other than my mum) who could connect me to that part of my heritage and culture, I was angry that I wasn't able to go into the temple. I was doubly angry as a budding feminist that it was my period, of all things, that was preventing me from connecting in some small but significant way to my heritage.

I found some kinder justifications about why women couldn't enter temples during their period, which focused on things like energy flows and the need to maintain the energetic and karmic balance of the temple. An alternative explanation is that the reason for the rule is because of menstrual taboos. Menstruation has long been associated with dirt, and disgust, and shame, and fear (Douglas 1966). Which is why I love that witches like Willow have deliberately carved out a space and a set of rituals and mythologies all centred around making sacred something that has been treated as taboo for hundreds of years by many cultures around the world.

The ways in which the Red Tent discourse refers to the stages of womanhood – maiden, mother and crone – can be considered a rite of passage, one that celebrates moving from childhood to adulthood (from maiden to mother) and from adulthood to elderhood (from mother to crone). Tying this rite of passage to bodily processes such as menstrual cycles and pregnancy deliberately pushes back against these deeply ingrained social taboos – taboos that are very effective at controlling how people move through spaces and what kinds of religious positions of power they can hold.

These taboos reflect what and who society values. Whether women are celebrated for their ability to procreate or damned for processes (like menstruation) that allow them to do so, both effectively bind women's value to their bodies. Both venerating them for their intimate knowledge and connection to nature, and shaming them for being dirty or unclean because of their bodies, shackles them to nature. Defining women as 'natural' because of their bodies or their knowledge of bodily processes (through healing crafts such as midwifery), whether those are in positive or negative terms, marries them to nature, and men to culture or civilization (Ortner 1974).

These questions continued to trouble me. Why is it that a religion such as witchcraft, which, from the outset, was determinedly controversial and countercultural, ends up reproducing (pun intended) the oppressive beliefs of the religious institutions it so vehemently opposes? My search for the answers to these questions took me far out of my comfort zone, away from Australia and halfway across the world to the crowded, sweaty, and never-ending party that is New Orleans.

5

The Death Witch

'My great grandmother was born in the cottage across the street from Marie Laveau.'
You can't really take a trip to New Orleans without hearing about the Voodoo Queen Marie Laveau. Which means I am not at all surprised when Camille tells me her version of Marie's infamous story and her personal connection to this legendary figure. Camille and I are sitting in the front room of her house, a classically French colonial house which has a parlour that Camille has converted into her very own altar room. Looking around, I noticed that in some ways it reminds me a little of my grandmother's house; she rarely threw things away and, over decades, the house had accumulated many knick-knacks, paintings, pictures and books.

Camille's knick-knacks were one of a kind. It was overwhelming to step into her altar room; every single wall was adorned with paintings or stacked high with ornaments. The fireplace was covered in candles and featured a discoloured and what looked to me like a real human skull. What caught my attention upon entering was a wooden column in the centre of the room that stretched almost all the way to the ceiling. The top was crowned in a chandelier-like creation of bright blue bottles that reflected the ceiling light. The effect was powerful; it created an ethereal celestial atmosphere in the top half of the room which clashed with the earthy, cluttered and swampy vibe of the rest of the room. The pedestal itself holding everything up was invisible, swamped by the many trinkets, including dried and hollowed-out gourds, letters, feathers, snake skins and, at the base of the column, a preserved alligator head.

Camille is a Voodoo priestess: a spiritual leader within the religion of Voodoo. Women in the New Orleans Voodoo tradition are believed to be the physical portal through which the loa, divinity and life itself descend from the invisible world. Camille was born and bred in New Orleans, a Louisiana native. She is not what I expected and at the same time exactly what I expected when I organized to meet with a Voodoo priestess. Her bright-red lips match the red claws she taps on her desk as she surveys me. Her smile reaches her searching eyes, she is doing what many witches before me have done before. I recognize the feeling now. They would observe my reactions to certain stories to see whether I was shocked or intrigued, but most of all, whether I took what they were saying seriously. They rightly wanted to know if I was there to fetishize their practices, or whether I genuinely cared about their deeply held beliefs.

But what makes a religion a religion? Is it having prayers to recite? Gods to listen to those prayers? For it to be called a religion, does it need to have a place of worship? Is it a legitimate religion if it's practised in someone's front room? In a hair salon? And what about the religious objects or artefacts? Is an alligator head as sacred as a holy communion cup?

The religion Camille practises is something she has developed and honed over decades. It's something she has taught to her own family, to her son and to priestesses in training, like Gina. In New Orleans, practising Voodoo within the city limits is believed by some to be illegal – most likely, a holdover from Jim Crow-era laws regulating when and where Black people could gather. You cannot talk about the history of New Orleans Voodoo without talking about race in the south. Now although the history of colonial New Orleans is too complex to rehash in full, there are a few important things to cover.

From the early eighteenth century, enslaved West Africans were forcibly brought to the French colony of Louisiana. While census data is not available for the slavery era of New Orleans, anecdotal evidence suggests the slave population constituted just over half the total population in Southern Louisiana. The status of a slave imposed a series of legal and social restrictions that excluded them from white society and all its privileges, including the freedom of religious expression.

The Atlantic slave trade forced the slaves to find ways of living in a context built on a foundation of their own enslavement. Voodoo offered an alternative way of being in America, of staying connected to Africa and carving out spaces of self-empowerment. Because Voodoo offered a means of accessing both culture and power, it represented a threat to the broader social order of the south. Voodoo was characterized at the time as ignorant, superstitious and childlike. This characterization (and denigration) of Voodoo in this light explains why it is now portrayed in popular culture as something dark (pun intended) and dangerous, wrapped up in zombies, dolls and animal sacrifice.

One of the main Voodoo characters or figures who appears in these depictions is Voodoo Queen Marie Laveau. Born in September 1794, Marie is arguably the most renowned Voodoo practitioner in the history of New Orleans. The legendary founder and priestess of American Voodoo was actually two women, a mother and daughter, who went by the same name. Both Maries were extraordinary women for their time; they were 'free women in a slave society, French

Catholics in an Anglo-Protestant nation, and *gens de couleur libre* – free people of color' (Ward 2004: ix). Marie Laveau continues to hold a powerful and enduring influence over the city of New Orleans.

From the way Camille leans back in her chair, I can tell the story she is about to relate is one she has not just memorized; it's part of who she is as a person. A part of the legacy of being a Voodoo priestess in New Orleans is to carry forward the story of Marie Laveau. Marie, she explained to me, is more than a historical or inspirational figure in Voodoo; she embodies the spirit of the tradition while also *being a spirit* who is called upon during ceremonies. She is also the perfect analogy for modern Voodoo as an originally devout Catholic, a free woman of colour and a spiritual leader of Voodoo. It is important to note that there is little archival evidence to back up the infamous stories about the Queen: from the exorcisms and love spells to the dances in Congo Square and the rituals on St John's Eve and curing of yellow fever victims during the Civil War (Magloire 2023).

Black feminist literary scholar Marina Magloire argues that in literature on New Orleans, Voodoo female leaders are referred to as Queens, while men are given the title of doctor. However, unlike most royal families, Voodoo Queens are not related by blood but through apprenticeships. I met Camille's apprentice Gina during a Voodoo tour of the French Quarter. Trundling through the cobbled streets, I sat in the front passenger seat and asked Gina about her relationship with Marie Laveau.

'When I was a kid, my parents took us to the New Orleans history museum and they had a wax exhibit of Marie Laveau. When I finally saw the image of her, I thought to myself how *beautiful* she was. I felt a connection. I felt that I belonged to her, and I wanted to grow up to be just like her. As a little kid I saw her and she became one of my heroes instantly, so I just gathered what I could here and there learning, and then found a house to join. I was initiated and went through all the rites and steps and became a priestess.'

Gina was not born to be a Queen; rather, she is learning what it means to be a Voodoo priestess through her apprenticeship with Camille – just like the priestess who seceded Marie Laveau, who was her apprentice, not one of her own daughters. Power in Voodoo is not passed down through bloodlines; rather, it is a craft that is acquired with time and dedicated practice and learning. I couldn't help but admire that level of faith.

Together, Camille and Gina were shattering all my previously held images of what a Voodoo priestess would look and sound like, which, in all honesty, had been informed primarily by Hollywood. This led me to ask Gina if the tourist industry had done much to either dispel or perpetuate misconceptions about Voodoo. 'I don't think it's the tourists that do that, I think it's Hollywood. They come here and they give Voodoo an evil reputation. It's always been that way. We are the most demonized religion and Hollywood is, I'd say, 90 per cent at fault. People only see Voodoo through TV and movies and it's always doing something bad.'

In popular culture, Voodoo is often portrayed as evil, morally grey at best. Its power is used primarily to manipulate and maim. While Voodoo is practised by men, women and nonbinary folk, it is Black women who are depicted as the Voodoo villains with harmful and frightening powers. In the 2005 horror film *Skeleton Key*, it is Mama Cecile who is the main villain, using the power of conjure to evade her own death, jumping from body to body and trapping poor souls along the way. The film is obviously not a faithful depiction of New Orleans Voodoo, nor does it do a fantastic job of handling the racial tensions of southern slavery and plantations. What the film does highlight, which I think is compelling and worth exploring further, is the power of *conjuring* in Voodoo.

The etymology of the word *conjure* is both fascinating and revealing, rooted in the Latin *coniurare*, which means 'to swear together; conspire'. Over the years, conjure evolved to become a verb that described some kind of invocation or summoning of magical power. In New Orleans Voodoo, conjure can also be a noun, used to describe someone as a conjure-woman. I became totally absorbed with this idea of conjuring, which led me to work on conjure feminism:

> Conjure feminism became a way to think specifically about the enduring histories of Black women's knowledge-production that began with the lessons we learned at our grandmothers' kitchen tables and are woven into the fabric of Black women's writing practices: motherwit, root medicine, food as ancestral memory, mothering, and spirit work. (Brooks et al. 2021: 456)

Black feminist literary scholars Kinitra Brooks, Kameelah Martin and LaKisha Simmons use the phrase 'conjure feminism' to capture and privilege this inherited wisdom. What I really loved about this concept is the focus on the places that have been claimed as part of this spiritual praxis, which are the extraordinarily everyday and everyday extraordinariness of homes, their gardens and their kitchens, and how such spaces are empowered not only by their knowledge, but also by that of their foremothers.

Don't forget to feed the dead

Witchcraft and Voodoo are distinct traditions, but the more time I spent with practitioners from both religions the more I was able to see the beliefs and practices they shared. They both, for example, place emphasis on working with, acknowledging and nourishing one's ancestors. One of my favourite rituals I observed involved feeding the ancestors. Camille's son and his girlfriend have been raised with Voodoo, which means it is not unusual for them to stop by the local shops to pick up fruits and candies to offer to the dead. But what happens to the food? Is it just left for the crows to enjoy? 'You let the spirits eat first and then you go ahead and eat the food and it's been blessed and you get some of the blessing from the spirits. Like for his grandma we went to do a ritual for her and brought snowballs with crème de mint because that was her favourite.'

Offering food to the dearly departed is not necessarily a new or unusual concept. It is a practice that appears in Hinduism. In this context it is a syncretic practice likely drawn from Indo- and Afro-Caribbean traditions. What differentiates this practice from, say, Christians leaving flowers at their loved ones' graves is how Voodoo practitioners conceptualize death. There's an exchange happening, an intimate reciprocity.

What it boils down to is that religion is about death: why it happens, our fear of its inevitability and uncertainty of when it will finally catch up with us. I was raised Catholic, which means I was taught to believe that when we die our bodies are left on earth to decay while our souls move on to some kind of afterlife, its nature dependent on our actions. This was reinforced for me as a young child when I attended my first funeral. During times of grief, adults often forget to sit down and explain to children what's happening, so they have to piece together for themselves what happened based on context. From my perspective, my aunty was still here: I could see her body when I attended the wake. What was missing was her presence. Her inappropriate jokes and stories she would tell at the dinner table. The figurines and bowls she hand-painted and gifted to my sister and myself. And then she was just gone. In the years that followed, we talked about her less and less and, when we did, it was in the past tense. There was a clear sense of finality when it came to the topic of death.

The years I spent with witches and Voodoo practitioners revealed to me an entirely different way of approaching death.

In Voodoo (and witchcraft), 'death is not an ending but a transition' (Brooks et al. 2021: 456). The dead do not ascend (or descend, depending on their actions during their lifetime) to a plane of existence inaccessible to the living. An afterlife that serves as a reward or punishment. Such thinking is characterized as transcendent, and applies to how God is thought of in religions such as Catholicism, as other-worldly and unknowable. In these types of faiths, it makes sense that their approach to life, to morality and death, would be linear. You're born, initiated into the faith, do (mostly) good things and, when you die, you are rewarded.

Voodoo and witchcraft reject the linearity of time, believing instead that it is something more complex and cyclical in nature. The past, present and future do not collapse in on one another; rather, they coexist. Spirits are located in the world of the living, able to interact and influence the lives of their offspring. This is something that is commonly observed in religions with largely immanent worldviews, meaning that the soul, or God, or whatever is held to be sacred, is not something separate from the 'world', but is contained and present within it. I should add a caveat here that no religion is entirely transcendent or immanent, with most containing elements that speak to both.

Gina pulls the van over to the first stop on our Voodoo tour of New Orleans, which of course is St Louis Cemetery No. 1, which features the tomb of Marie Laveau. It is no surprise that this is our first stop; you can't tell the story of New Orleans Voodoo and not talk about the Queen of Voodoo herself. 'When you're brought up in New Orleans, of course Voodoo is a big part of the culture here; everywhere it's in music, food, it's in everything', Gina said, turning off the engine and twisting in her seat to address everyone in the back of the van. Behind us are Camille and two other tour attendees. Gina is running the show, but I can see Camille is watching her carefully, ensuring the stories are told right, in the right order with the right tone.

Making sure she makes the correct stops along the way. And, of course, ready to step in with various and often dramatic interjections of her own. It's an engaging performance. I have no doubt they believe the things they are saying, the histories they carry forward. But there is a flamboyant and effervescent air to their storytelling.

'Marie's spirit has been seen by people not just near her tomb but all-around town. It's something people come to New Orleans in search of, to catch a glimpse of her', Gina says in her deep New Orleans twang, with just a hint of spookiness. I can see from the offerings around Marie's tomb that many people had indeed come in search of the Voodoo Queen, almost 130 years after her death. The white tomb is adorned (or graffitied, depending on your point of view) with messages. The most popular of these are crosses made in sets of three using red bricks and charcoal, meant to be part of people's pilgrimage to the tomb, a way of honouring Marie and asking her for help. The front of the tomb has amassed a collection of offerings for the Voodoo Queen: colourful Mardi Gras beads, whole cakes, pineapples and oranges, flowers, candles, letters and even a few bottles of alcohol. The collection is arranged at the foot of the temple like an altar. Some of the items have been placed there recently, their colours still vibrant. Others have begun to fade, colours dropping out of the beads, petals falling, fruit beginning to rot in the sun and cake crumbling away in the humidity.

This is not the same as the holy communion and wine, which are kept behind lock and key by a select few members of the clergy and served in golden plates and cups. There was a distinct sense of materiality and decay to this form of religiosity. Now, one could ask what religious beliefs are being expressed in material form. But a much more interesting question concerns how religion happens materially. Which means paying attention to the material stuff in religious practices and the power of things, bodies and places.

What I noticed is that it wasn't just Voodoo practitioners who were paying their respects at the tomb of Marie Laveau. It was everyday residents and tourists. And they were using a variety of offerings to enter into a relationship with the Voodoo Queen. These offerings were not intended to be long-lasting; in fact, they are meant to fall apart, to fade in the sun and eventually decay. The material nature of these objects, their decomposition, is not inconsequential. It creates a sense of obligation on the part of visitors, Voodoo practitioners, locals and tourists alike. These objects, these things, become active through the ways they are prepared, offered and eventually decay. It feels as though there is a sense of deep care and devotion in this religious practice. This relationship to the divine in Voodoo is reciprocal, as opposed to the covenant relationship to the divine in Christianity.

It reminded me of what Camille's son had told me, about his family bringing his grandmother's favourite food to offer to her. To feed her. To feed someone whether they are your child, a friend or departed relative is to show that you care for them. That you love them. This helps to maintain relationships and the presence of the dead within established kin relationships and therefore more broadly in society. Something that would be considered taboo from a Christian point of view.

Love, longing and loas

In Voodoo, I learned along our tour, there are different types of ancestors. Witches make a similar distinction between the mighty dead and the beloved dead. The beloved dead are witches' blood relatives, whereas the mighty dead are witches who have died with no direct familial connection. Either may be called upon during rituals. Marie Laveau therefore would represent one of the mighty dead, an ancestor whom many in New Orleans (and beyond) call upon.

The mighty dead are called loa in New Orleans Voodoo. Linguists argue that the word comes from a family of Yoruba language words which include *olúwa* (god) and *babalawo* (which means diviner or priest). Also spelt lwa, it may also come from the French term for law, *loi*, and a Haitian Creole term for law, *lwa*. Given the French colonial history of New Orleans, this is not entirely surprising.

French Catholicism has had an enduring influence on New Orleans Voodoo. This connection became clearer to us as we arrived at the final location of our tour – Camille's home. Standing in the parlour in front of the wooden column, she explained how the loas act as intermediaries between people and the ancestors. Gesturing at the base of the column, she explained how 'the base represents the earthly realm, where we live, moving up is both the loa and how they communicate with us'; waving at the roof at the collection of blue bottles, she says they 'represent the realm of the gods'. A beautiful and straightforward symbol of Voodoo cosmology.

When the slaves from Senegal, the Bight of Benin and the Congo region were forcibly and violently removed from their home and taken across the Atlantic Ocean, they were forbidden from practising their own religious beliefs. Since the dominant religion during this period was Catholicism, the African slaves merged their gods and spirits with the saints. This way they could practise their religion safely, a necessary means of survival. This blending process is also referred to as creolization, when elements of different cultures are brought together and create a new culture.

For example, one spirit unique to New Orleans Voodoo (in comparison to the Haitian variant) is 'St. Marron, the patron saint of enslaved runaways who communicates with practitioners through snakes' (Clark 2020: 144). These spirits possess the bodies of Voodoo practitioners and act as intermediaries between the human world and the realm of the supernatural.

Gina explained how, 'once you are in the right mode or ritual form, the loa gives you messages and guidance. In dreams and in rituals they visit you and connect with you. What we practise was also practised in ancient times'. In modern times only a priest can have such a connection to God or a saint. In Voodoo one earns religious authority through their connection to the spirit world. She goes on to explain: 'Like I was saying with the ancestors, loas is the term in general for gods in Voodoo so you have like your local loa or just people who you pray to and she [Marie Laveau] was one of the great spirits: she gets offerings and she's prayed to for help just like any other loa or any ancestors.'

'Could I pray to Marie?' I thought to myself. She was a big part of what had drawn me to the Crescent in the first place. Her legend and her power. Her resistance to every form of oppression and social control. A free woman of colour, openly practising a forbidden religion, one that connected her to her ancestors. A practice that bestowed power and authority to women. Priestess. Witch.

All of these were names for what I was searching for, a connection to something that was beyond myself. I realized when I booked the tickets to come here that I was fulfilling the typical break-up pattern of using a trip to avoid feeling and dealing. Unfortunately, personal problems don't play nice and stay home while you take a vacation; they have a habit of following you and showing up at inopportune times. All this talk about offerings and connecting with the dead made me feel as though I might be able to connect with Marie in my own way. To ask her for help in making sense of my life now it all has been flipped on its head.

Hair, grief and gossip

It's been a few months since I arrived in New Orleans. After living in the city for a few months, I've adjusted to the heavy humidity that never seems to fade even when night falls. I've decided to visit Camille at her house, to talk to her about my desire to make an offering to Marie. She greets me at the door and, rather than taking me into her altar room as I anticipated, she takes me down the narrow hallway. The high walls are covered in an eclectic collection of artwork. Noticing that my attention had been drawn to the paintings, she points to a collection of small floral patterns and asks if I like this selection.

'I do', I say automatically; obviously I'm not going to insult someone's taste in artwork in their own home. 'Look closer', she says. Peering closer, I could see they were not simply paintings of flowers, but what appeared to be dried flowers pressed into bunches mounted with pins like butterflies. 'Yes, I can see the flowers', I replied, smiling politely, 'very pretty.' 'Can you tell what they're made of?', she asked, a knowing grin stretching across her face. Frowning, I leaned in closer. It was human hair. Delicate strands of brown and black hairs woven together carefully into flowers. Leaning back, I felt a little bit repulsed. Why would someone have pictures of human hair decorating the hallway of their home?

Smiling at both my realization and confusion, Camille explained to me that the Victorian practice of hair art had made its way to the banks of the Mississippi during one of many waves of colonization New Orleans underwent. 'This is how women kept their hands busy while they were grieving', she explained. For the Victorians, hairwork is a craft that creates artefacts such as framed pictures or jewellery from the hair of loved ones who had died: 'Artefacts of beloved bodies still held some of the sublime, fetishistic magic of those outmoded holy relics of bygone days. Not only does death bring the tragedy of turning people into things – of subject into object – but it might also start inanimate objects to life' (Lutz 2011: 128). The practice of hairwork, the remnants of which decorate the hall of Camille's House of Voodoo, is an example of contagious magic. The threads of hair moving between the fingers of the grieving mother tethers her to her child, reaching across the veil that separates the living and the dead.

Hairwork was heavily influenced by Romantic emotional and Evangelical revival in the 1930s and '40s and the rise of spiritualism in the 1950s and '60s. Spiritualists believed that the worlds of the living and the dead, the absent and the present, were permeable and accessible through seances, table-tapping and special photography (Lutz 2011: 132). Contact with the spiritual world was not just a hopeful pastime of the bereaved. Spiritualism may have been a soothing source of consolation when it began, but it morphed into an ethereal engine of confidence for many of the women who practised it. The messages of self-worth and female independence missing in their mundane lives were found in the voices of the dead. The practice of hairwork on one level gave women something to keep them busy rather than falling into despair. The practice also expresses a deeper desire to approach death as it permeates life, to be intimate with death in a way that, on the one hand, is spiritual and, on the other, is material.

Hair-braiding is a practice found in almost every culture. It is a craft that takes both time and patience to master. Like a lot of other people, indeed like a lot of other women, I learned to braid my hair when I was young, from my mother. Sitting at her knee she would use a wet brush to tame my thick and curly hair into a neat weave. Unlike my mother, who grew up in Fiji where curly hair was celebrated, I grew up in Australia in the 1990s and spent most of the early years of my life furiously trying to straighten my hair.

I knew my hair was very much like my mother's when she was young. Her wedding photo showed off her long thick curls. But like many other women who have their first child, she had cropped it short – one less thing for her to think about. Taking my hair between her hands she pulls apart three sections and begins weaving one under the other. I would often practise my braiding at the weekends, annoyed when it did not turn out looking as neat as hers, the braids often falling out much sooner. I would admire the girls at school with their beautiful intricate blonde hair twisted artfully into French braids decorated with butterfly clips. I began to hate my hair from a very early age. I hated the halo of baby curls and frizz that would escape and frame my face, and I detested the waves that made my braids look 'messy'. Straightening my hair began in high school and continued for many years afterwards – a ritual of discipline, using extreme heat to tame my curls.

Hair is a highly symbolic part of the body and Black feminist theorists have written for decades about the politics of hair, about white aesthetics, constructions of race, skin colour, self-esteem, ritual, beauty and identity. Ever since my ritual with Fae I had developed a fascination with magical practices and beliefs about hair. In the context of New Orleans, this obsession led me right back to the Voodoo Queen. A major part of the lore about Marie Laveau is that she financially supported herself by becoming a hairdresser, and this was how she accumulated her social capital and influence – by tending to the hair of wealthy white women and learning their secrets (Alvarado 2020).

Gossip as a practice of survival has been written about in the specific cultural and social context of hair salons owned and frequented by African American women. Marie Laveau is one of the most infamous examples of this. Shortly after the death of her husband, according to both local legend and historical records, Laveau became a hairdresser, catering to the wealthy white and Creole women of New Orleans. According to locals, many of these women looked upon Marie as a confidante, confessing to her their most intimate secrets and desires. In addition to gaining economic freedom, Laveau reportedly used the gossip she gathered from her hairdressing business to accumulate considerable social power. She was able to influence political decisions in a local sense, for example, to allow free Black people and slaves to congregate and dance in Congo Square, which was previously illegal under the Code Noir.[12] Laveau's social power continued to grow and extend, reaching far beyond the space of her beauty salon.

Historians like Tiffany Gill (2010) have written extensively about the vital role beauty salons played in civil rights activism. Gill argues that 'the black beauty industry must be understood as providing one of the most important opportunities for black women to assert leadership in their communities and the larger political arena' (2010: 20). As I am writing this chapter, the Taliban have issued an order to close beauty shops in Afghanistan, effectively denying Afghan women the means of earning an income and connecting with one another (Mukhtar 2023). In each of these examples, we can see the process of economic enclosure as it is directly tied to the devaluation of women's work and deliberate disintegration of their social ties. Gossip, in these settings, has the potential to be mobilized in order to actively resist dominant structures of political power and control. Media and cultural studies scholar Andrew Navin Brooks describes this type of gossip as a form of fugitive listening:

> [Gossip] is a form of radical knowledge that moves outside of official discourse, circulating noisy information across a social body. As such, we can make a historical distinction between modes of idle talk that affirm and uphold the dominant sociopolitical order – such as the locker-room talk of influential men – and gossip, a mode of speech that has evolved as a way to circumvent the dismissal of certain voices as noise. Indeed,

---

12 In 1724, the French colony introduced a series of cruel and repressive acts governing the behaviour of slaves, known as *Code Noir*. These legal restrictions included the restrictions around religious participation and performances.

the refusal to hear gossip as speech is, paradoxically, what gives rise to its interruptive potentiality. (2020: 39)

Historically and cross-culturally, gossip has been portrayed as idle women's talk and something that is harmful to others. The negative connotations attached to gossip are not accidental; rather, they are a result of a broader capitalist and colonial design intended to silence and control particular groups of people.

The words 'godparent' and 'gossip' both come from the same pair of Old English terms – *god* and *sibb*. The term first emerged in the twelfth century and almost always referred to women, since they were usually the ones attending during childbirth. The women would spend hours in conversations with one another, sharing stories and knowledge about motherhood and reproductive health. These affairs were incredibly social and attended exclusively by women. Over time, *gossip* evolved from a noun used to describe the companions of a woman during childbirth to a verb that referred to a meeting of female friends.

Gossip circles more closely resembled salon gatherings, where women would gather to discuss personal matters such as marriage, and also political issues. Since men were excluded from these social spaces and conversations, gossip began to develop a negative connotation. This first began when the term 'gossip' began to appear in a series of plays. During the fifteenth and sixteenth centuries, plays were the modern-day equivalent of popular television shows, in that they were a form of entertainment for the masses. Popular forms of entertainment can be very useful for revealing the fears and anxieties of the time. In this case, they alluded to fears about women and the social power they held. The plays portrayed women as 'gossips' who would gather in taverns to drink wine and complain about their husbands. These women were painted as aggressive, quick to start fights with their husbands and willing to engage in a 'battle for the breeches' (Federici 2018: 76) – the modern-day equivalent of fighting for 'who wears the pants?', a joke I have heard at far too many weddings in my lifetime.

Covens, conspiracies and colonialism

The shift of the word 'gossip' from a morally neutral term to a negative one didn't just happen by mere accident; there were much broader social and economic changes at play that caused this change to occur. Silvia Federici explains how this change occurred during a significant period of transition for women, when they held a considerable amount of social capital even though their position in public spaces was increasingly under threat (Federici 2018: 75). For example, the guilds that were organizing and funding the plays were made up of merchants and craftsmen, who were primarily interested in accumulating their own political and economic power. Gossips become the vehicle for ridiculing women in these plays as a means of reinforcing their preferred social order and norms, with women confined to private spaces such as the home and subservient to the men in their life, such as their father or husband.

Many of the plays portrayed scenes from the Bible. However, as historian Hetta Elizabeth Howes (2024) attests, these representations were far from accurate. The guilds used a fair amount of creative licence in their work, such as portraying Noah as a drunken fool and his wife as a shrewish nag. The combination of humour and the novelty of seeing your neighbours or your local baker appearing in such epic tales as Noah's Ark or the Crucifixion were a crucial part of the plays' popularity. The popularity of the plays and the wealth of the guild members combined proved to be an influential force. Guild members' desire to move up the social ladder required a commitment to upholding some behaviours, while admonishing others. This is why gossip became the target of ridicule in these plays, because it was an effective and humorous way of belittling women without being overly conspicuous.

Portraying women as gossips was not the only way of humiliating and silencing them at this time. There were more brutal forms of torture that emerged – for example, the scold's bridle was a form of punishment for women deemed 'quarrelsome' or 'troublesome' or 'riotous'. Also known as the witch's, or the gossip's, bridle, this instrument took the form of an iron mask with a bridle 'bit', like a horse bit, that slid into the wearer's mouth to silence them. While the scold's bridle is an obvious form of physical torture, the psychological and broader social effects were much more insidious. Imagine being a woman during these times and seeing your friends, your neighbours, being forced to wear the scold's bridle in public. The fear of this happening to you should you be accused of being a gossip or quarrelsome with your husband would have been made even more real and immediate.

The first documented appearance of the scold's bridle was in Scotland where it was used on those who committed blasphemy. It made it easier to justify this brutal use of torture under the guise of religion. This is one of the reasons – I believe – that the scold's bridle was also called the gossip's bridle. On the surface, it was an obvious way of preventing and punishing someone for gossiping. However, digging a little deeper we find more complex reasons at play. Our first clue is in the way gossip is described as 'idle talk'. On the one hand, it's an effective way of classifying women's words as meaningless. On the other, it is a means of signalling that gossip is a sin, therefore those who gossip are sinful.

If you have ever found yourself taking a break during the work day and felt a sense of guilt for being lazy and unproductive, please allow me to introduce you to why this is not because you lack a strong 'work ethic'. For the most part, the reason laziness and idleness has such a chokehold on the way we work is because of certain Protestant beliefs that were later adopted by the Puritans. Scholar of English literature Monika Fludernik argues that 'early modern (Puritan) notions about the sinfulness of idleness and the necessity of constant labour remained prominent despite the increasing secularization of British society' (2017: 133). This is obviously not restricted to British society. Capitalism adopted and circulated the idea that labour improved one's moral character and this idea was exported throughout the British empire. It should therefore not come as a surprise then that the scold's bridle was used both on quarrelsome women accused of gossiping and to silence and control slaves in America.

What does the use of these mechanisms of humiliation tell us about the people using them? That they were scared shitless of what could happen if those who did not receive equal benefits in the prevailing regime, whether that be feudalism or capitalism, got together and started to talk. One of the ways this manifested itself was in the fear of *covens* of witches. What is the power of an individual witch compared to the potential threat of a collective of witches – a coven? A coven is a group or gathering of witches; the word is Anglo-Norman in its origins, stemming from the Latin *conventus*, meaning 'assembly, company'. We can see from historical accounts that the idea of witches being collectively organized was something that struck fear into the hearts of the clergy (Summers 2011: 108–9) and the emerging middle class (Federici 2018: 61). Many of the trials and confessions focused on organizational details, from how many witches were in the coven, to how often they met, to whether there were leaders within the group.

Talking can lead to anger. Anger can lead to action. Actions can lead to riots. Riots can lead to revolts. This is where Marie Laveau's real power stemmed from. Not her knowledge of ritual or ceremony (even though these were still important). It was her knowledge, the secrets she accumulated from the middle- and upper-class women she had in her salon chair. She knew who was hiding illicit affairs and she used that information (allegedly) to challenge oppressive policies that restricted the freedoms and movement of Black folks in New Orleans.

Meeting Marie

It's my last few days in New Orleans and I still haven't made it to Marie's tomb by myself. I finally found the courage to make an offering of my own after a conversation I had with a Voodoo priestess I met swimming one day in my hostel. From the outside, the hostel looked quite glamorous, pale pink with white columns and verandas wrapping around the front. On closer inspection, you could tell the colonial mansion had seen better days. Paint peeling inside, ancient and astoundingly loud air-conditioning units in the individual rooms. I decided against bunking with others and forked out for an individual room. The place was cheap to live in long term while I was researching Voodoo, plus it had a wicked vibe and a nice big pool to lounge in on the especially humid days. Dropping my notebook and bag in my room, I quickly changed into a bikini so I could catch the last hour of sunshine.

Shimming into the pool, I let out a sigh of relief; the humidity of the Crescent city was not something I would miss upon my return to Australia. Looking up, I noticed two young women I had become friends with over the months. One day I was curious about why they were always in the pool in the middle of the day. Were they out here doing fieldwork like myself, or just on a ridiculously long extended holiday? Turns out they were strippers working in the clubs on Bourbon Street.

I loved watching them somewhat voyeuristically when they interacted with others from the hostel, like the boys they flirted with so openly while lounging by the pool or breaking into a slow sensual dance to whatever music someone happened to be playing from their speaker. This time they had someone new with them. Smiling at them, I slowly paddled my way over to meet their new friend. 'Oh my god, Hannah, you HAVE to meet Emma, she's come all the way from Australia and she's researching Voodoo', one of the dancers said. Well that did about sum up what I was here for. Hannah smiled at me. I admired the freckles on her nose that gathered together when she laughed, I also noticed her arms were covered in trad-style tattoos. 'Well it's lovely to meet you Emma', Hannah said, grinning at me in a friendly and inviting way. 'What brought you here in the first place?'

Despite being a total stranger, something about Hannah made me feel at ease. Our mutual friends had slinked off to the other side of the pool to chat to a couple of German lads who had joined our pool party, the water droplets on their backs glistening in the sun. Hannah and I were alone, in a sense, in our end of the pool – at least, we were out of the earshot of the other people present. Strangely, it felt almost as if I was in a priest's confession. I told her about my research into Voodoo, about how I wanted to understand how a religion shaped over the years by many waves of colonial violence, and set in a country that is less than kind to women, came to be. One that venerates women from history, like Marie Laveau, and elevates women to high places of religious authority. I also told her about my breakup. About the heartache I carried in my chest everywhere I went, how confused and ultimately scared I was about the future. All the plans we had made together, all the promises to love one another forever that had evaporated. What is going to happen now? How am I supposed to know the right thing to do? And more importantly, who even am I?

'Sounds like Marie whispered to you, she was what brought you here', Hannah said kindly.

'I guess so', I said. 'She's so strong and powerful, I've admired her since I was a teenager', I admitted.

'I don't think you're lost at all,' she said. 'You're here aren't you? Following your passion, your desire to know more. Have you gone to visit her?' she asked.

'I've been to her tomb, but it was part of a tour and with a group of people,' I said.

'You should go see her,' Hannah encouraged. 'It doesn't need to be elaborate, just take something to give to her and have a conversation.'

So I finally did. I caught a bus from outside my hostel to the St Louis Cemetery No. 1 the very next morning. I decided to take some of my favourite treats from my time in New Orleans, sweet tea and beignets. More than a little touristy, and predictable, but delicious nonetheless. I chose a Tuesday morning to avoid the usual crowds later in the week and was delighted to find only a small crowd around her tomb. Out of respect for her family, who had erected signs asking visitors not to mark her tomb, I chose not to leave a message on the wall, opting instead to gently place my sweet tea and packet of beignets among the other offerings on the steps in front of her tomb. Grateful that the sun was not in full force, I lingered at the back of the crowd, looking around at the other above ground tombs in the cemetery. Camille and Gina had explained to us during our tour a few months back that New Orleans is at, or below, sea level, resulting in a high water table in the soil. If a body or coffin is placed in an in-ground tomb in New Orleans, there is a risk of it being water-logged or even displaced from the ground. There was something beautiful and profound about this. The spatiality of cemeteries was completely shaped by this environmental necessity; it felt like you were walking through the houses of New Orleans ancestors. Rather than returning them to the earth, it felt like they were still here. Sitting in these tiny houses like tombs, waiting for us to visit and talk to them.

Visiting Marie felt like calling on one of the big guns, the heavyweight champion of the ancestors. The mighty dead.

Sucking in some deep breaths of humid air, I closed my eyes briefly. 'Marie', I thought to myself, 'I don't know what to do with this feeling in my chest. Sometimes I have to stop what I'm doing, making eggs or putting my socks on just to cry. I cry all the time but this is different, it's like I can't breathe and I'm afraid to stop because when I do I have to deal with the fact it's over. He doesn't love me anymore, and after everything he told me no one ever will. I'm too needy. Too horny. Too slutty. Too talkative. Too much full stop. I'm not just scared of being alone, I'm scared no one will ever love me. The real me, not the version I cut myself down into just to please him.'

Opening my eyes after saying my not-prayer prayer in my head I realized that a few tears had escaped despite my efforts to contain them. Slipping on my sunglasses, I looked up at her tomb and felt some of the pressure on my chest ease. I had finally done it, admitting to myself what I was really scared of: on the one hand, I was grieving the loss of the relationship but, on the other, I was also grieving the loss of my identity. The one I had wrapped around him, in having a partner and therefore being valued. For me, being with someone made me someone. Never mind how that person treated me or made me feel about myself.

This was the perfect liminal space to allow this part of myself, my identity, to (symbolically) die. It was time, time to forgive myself for giving away the pieces of myself over the years. It was also time to go get those pieces back and love them as much as I deserved to be loved. An important part of this forgiveness involved allowing myself to feel angry, white hot rage coursing through my body. Which is what led me to perform my very first hex.

6

The Techno Witch

'Beginner friendly, simple hex'

I had the sudden realization while scrolling through my phone, submitting to the oblivion of the TikTok For You Page (FYP), that well over half of the videos I was watching were all of witches performing hexes. And like any good (read here: manipulative) algorithm, the more I watched, the more videos it showed me. *Hex.* The idea had a dark glamour to it; this word and the rituals it inspired gave me a sense of comfort almost, like a perverse mantra. I began to think about hexes obsessively: what forms they could take, what it might mean to perform one.

For close to a year, my TikTok and Instagram connections became almost completely devoted to hexes. I would open the apps and would be immediately greeted by witches demonstrating the best ways to go about performing binding spells, cord-cutting rituals and putting together sour jar hexes on their exes. The most recent hex to come across my FYP was one cast on American far-right political pundit and misogynist Nick Fuentes, who had tweeted the misogynist rallying cry: 'Your body, my choice.' He also stated publicly that 'we need to revive the witch hunts of old' and 'go back to burning women alive'. These outright calls for gendered violence have inspired witches to hex Nick, with one TikTok video garnering more than a million views.

Many attribute the origins of these particular types of hexes to a binding spell that went viral in 2017, 'A Spell to Bind Donald Trump and All Those Who Abet Him', which was originally created by Michael M. Hughes. The spell received a large amount of media attention and was performed by high-profile participants, including Lana Del Rey:

> Yeah, I did it. Why not? Look, I do a lot of shit. There's a power to the vibration of a thought. Your thoughts are very powerful things and they become words, and words become actions, and actions lead to physical changes ... I really do believe that words are one of the last forms of magic and I'm a bit of a mystic at heart. (Bryant 2017: n.p.)

As these very public and political hexes began unfolding on social media, I found myself asking why it is that witches and feminists (and witchy feminists) reach for hexes for their political activism. What actually is a hex and does it hold any actual power?

To the casual observer, it might seem like the Trump binding spell was the catalyst that kicked off a number of high-profile online hexes, such as those performed on Supreme Court Justice Brett Kavanaugh and Stanford rapist Brock Turner. And while it is true that the spell to bind Trump did go viral and inspired the subsequent hexes on high-profile creeps, politically motivated and public hexes have a much longer history in witchcraft than most people realize.

A conspiracy from hell

Imagine it's Halloween and you've just stopped by your favourite coffee shop on your way to work. The air is crisp this morning and, as you pull your thick scarf around your neck, you notice the usual noise of the morning commuters is punctuated by an unusual and repetitive chant: *'Wall Street, Wall Street, Crookedest Street of All Street, Foreign Exchange, Student Exchange, Wife Exchange, Stock Exchange, Trick or Treat, Up Against the Wall Street!'* The lyrics stop you in your tracks as you and others around you look to discover the source of the song. And then you see them. The coven of women, costumed as shamans, fairy queens, matriarchal old sorceresses, and witches dancing and twirling their way down Wall Street.

It's 1968 and members of W.I.T.C.H. (the Women's International Terrorist Conspiracy from Hell) have just descended on the New York financial district in their first ever protest. In an act of playful and public civil disobedience, W.I.T.C.H. danced to the Federal Reserve Treasury Bank, led by a High Priestess holding the papier mâché head of a pig aloft on a golden platter. They marched together to the New York Stock Exchange and, in front of a two-hundred-strong crowd, gathered to create a sacred circle and proclaimed the coming demise of stocks. This is how one of the founders of W.I.T.C.H., Robin Morgan, described the first public demonstration of this radical feminist group in her 1977 memoir *Going Too Far: The Personal Chronicle of a Feminist*. Fast forward a year, W.I.T.C.H. also attended a protest organized by various feminist groups, to demonstrate against the inauguration of Richard Nixon as President of the United States (Echols 2019). So, you see, witches gathering to protest and resist conservative and misogynist public figures is not such a new trend.

The first W.I.T.C.H. group was established in New York City in October 1968. Its founders were socialist feminists who had formerly been members of the New York Radical Women group. They opposed the idea advocated by radical feminists that feminist women should campaign against 'patriarchy' in isolation. The collective was created to expose *capitalism* and not men, as the real enemy of American women. Socialist anarchists.

What I find interesting is the group's deliberate decision to weaponize the disruptive potential of the witch. Religious studies scholar Cynthia Eller argues that, by choosing this symbol, 'feminists were identifying themselves with everything women were taught not to be: ugly, aggressive, independent, and malicious'. She goes on to explain that feminists like members of W.I.T.C.H. reached for this symbol, reclaimed it and shaped it 'into a symbol of female power, knowledge, independence, and martyrdom' (1993: 55). This martyrdom is most clearly visible in one of the chants W.I.T.C.H. used, which was 'Nine Million Women, Burned as Witches'. This idea draws directly from the myth of the matriarchal prehistory promoted, as I've discussed previously. Today, this sentiment has been capitalized on in contemporary feminist groups that draw on these same narratives. If you were to search on Etsy for witchy merchandise, you can find bundles of posters and t-shirts branded with the popular slogan: 'We are the granddaughters of the witches you couldn't burn.'

Putting to one side the irony of the sentiments spread (in part) by a socialist radical feminist group being literally capitalized on, what's more important to note here is the legacy of hexes and curses being deliberately used as political performance and protest. A more fundamental question to ask is: Why are people afraid of women who cast hexes?

A brief look at hexes, curses and 'white magic'

Witches have long been associated with powers to harm or cause chaos. The English word 'hex' itself is derived from the German word *Hexe*, used to describe a witch or a curse (Sayer

2009: 250). A hex (or a curse) is a spell that is intended to bring misfortune to a specific person. Hexes can be attached to objects like the Annabelle doll from *The Conjuring* film franchise. Or it can be cast from afar using a representation of the intended victim or victims. Accusations of casting hexes on others, on their crops or livestock, goes far back, to the witch hunts of the fifteenth to seventeenth centuries in Europe.

Hexes have played a significant role in human history, often transcending cultural and religious boundaries. In ancient Egypt, Greece and Rome, curses were inscribed on tablets or objects to bring harm or misfortune to the intended target. These hexes were believed to possess supernatural powers and were typically invoked for personal vengeance or to protect one's interests. The glorious 1999 cinematic masterpiece *The Mummy* is a prime example of this type of curse. After betraying the Pharaoh, high priest Imhotep is tortured, cursed and buried alive. The film took inspiration from the idea of the 'curse of the mummy' that circulated around the 1922 discovery of King Tutankhamun's tomb in the Valley of the Kings near Luxor, Egypt. While the film employs more fantastical details than what unfolded in real life, the sentiment remains the same. Archaeologists and other explorers discover a mummy's tomb, ignoring said warnings inscribed on the walls of the pyramid, on the Book of the Dead and on the tomb itself. After the team reads aloud the curse of the mummy the curse is activated. Hijinks ensue.

Growing up in the 1990s, I was a big fan of this movie, and as a result I was always too scared to mess around with hexes. But it wouldn't be fair to blame the film entirely for this fear. I was also raised on a steady diet of witchy millennial classics like *Charmed*, *Buffy the Vampire Slayer* and *Practical Magic*. Their makers openly borrowed elements from contemporary witches, like casting circles, calling on the elements and ancestor worship. They also inadvertently absorbed some of the beliefs and inner anxieties of witches of the time. For example, the emphasis on 'light and love' or 'white witchcraft' over so-called black witchcraft – possibly a hangover from the movement's development alongside New Age spirituality. I also think it came from a desire to rebrand witchcraft's image. To smooth out the edges and make witchcraft more palatable for public consumption.

The symbol of the witch still carries associations with what Federici calls 'the bad witch', she 'who curses and lames cattle and ruins crops' (2004: 338). In addition to causing these forms of chaos and misfortune that affect the production of food for the village, witches were also believed to perform certain acts that were directly tied to sexuality: having sex with incubi, carrying out abortions, causing sterility and stillbirth, and impeding sexual relations between husbands and wives (Smith 2002). Whether it was about reproduction or producing food, the witch represented a threat to the social order, specifically, the social order that feudal lords and the Church were attempting to establish.

Historian Ann Barstow calls attention to the fact that women who used herbs for healing, delivering babies or performing abortions, predicting the future, cursing others or removing curses, were vulnerable to witchcraft accusations. This is because these women were performing functions that 'overlapped dangerously with the priest's job' (1994: 109). One of my favourite stories about the dangers and so-called powers of witchcraft comes from the *Malleus Maleficarum*. During the late mediaeval period in Europe, beliefs about witches causing impotence were plentiful. An infamous example was the belief that witches could make the old one-eyed snake disappear. There were a number of specific examples in which witches were said to have mystically deprived men of their beloved appendages. In the *Malleus Maleficarum*, Heinrich Kramer describes one man's quest to restore his missing member. According to this account, the poor, castrated fellow 'approached a certain witch' who instructed him to 'climb a particular tree where there was a nest containing many members, and ... to take any one he liked' (Mackay and Institoris 2009: 328). After trying to choose the largest one in the nest, which he was denied, the witch informing him (in my head I imagine her sniggering as she did so) that he could not take that particular member because 'it belonged to a parish priest'.

The fear of female castration is a subject that has been well researched. For instance, feminist film theorist Barbara Creed (2023: 14–15) argues that when the feminine is fabricated as monstrous, it is commonly achieved through association with (female) reproductive bodily functions, or through matriarchal traits and tasks. She draws on Julia Kristeva's (1982) theory of abjection to challenge the popular view that women in horror movies are almost always victims, arguing that patriarchal ideology constructs women as monstrous in relation to their sexuality and reproductive body to justify their subjugation.

Creed explores the monstrous figure of the witch through the 1976 film *Carrie*, the plot of which most of us are familiar with due to the infamous pig's blood scene at the prom. Carrie's powers of telekinesis are awakened because of her tormentors both at school and at home, all of which can be tied back to her experiencing her first menses, also known colloquially as *the curse*. Creed argues that the film represents Carrie as both a witch and a menstrual monster and that, by 'associating Carrie's supernatural powers with blood, the film draws on superstitious notions of the terrifying powers of menstrual blood' (2023: 79). The film draws on the long history of associating witches with the disruption of social order – in the case of Carrie, her own family's implosion seeps outwards to destroy her entire high school community which is blamed on her own bodiliness, her leaky and lustful body. In Carrie's case, her curse is twofold. There is the curse of her menstruation, and the curse of becoming a young woman with wants and desires. Creed proposes a new concept of *radical abjection* to reinterpret the monstrous-feminine as a figure who embraces abjection by reclaiming her body and redefining her otherness as nonhuman, while questioning patriarchy, anthropocentrism and misogyny. Groups that embrace forms of magical resistance, like W.I.T.C.H. and their contemporaries, are drawing on a radical definition of the figure of the witch, one that draws power from its liminal position to resist oppression and control.

A witch who cannot hex cannot heal

Resisting oppression and control resonates strongly with women today, with reproductive rights under threat with the overturning of Roe v. Wade and the re-election of a convicted sexual predator to the highest office in the US. Both within and beyond America, the far right has been emboldened by Trump's re-election, and now we're seeing an even more brazen form of misogyny slithering into the open on social media.

For example, Nick Fuentes's tweet 'Your body, my choice' enraged witches on social media, who began sharing ideas for hexes to cast on him. One TikTok that garnered more than a million views features Delilah Bon's song 'Dead Men Don't Rape', a ferocious punk and nu-metal song. While the TikTok only features the chorus where Delilah screams over razor-wire guitar riffs, 'Dead Men Don't Rape', there are some other lyrics that I think are even more pertinent to the disruptive power that hexes represent:

> Maybe it is and they're scared we'll discover
> The strength of our feminine power
> The strength of our anger in numbers
> We are the witches they burned at the stake.

The popular symbol of the witch hunt – the woman burning at the stake – is invoked by both the far left (as seen in Delilah's lyrics) and also by the far right, as we can see in Nick Fuentes's own words:

> We need to go back to burning women alive. Like when they're convicted of crimes obviously. Not-not random acts of violence. But remember that in medieval times I've said this on the show before. When women were witches, what happened to them? They were burned alive. Real phenomenon. And we stopped doing that and then everything went out of control.

This certainly isn't the first time political figures have called on witches or the witch hunt trope for their own nefarious ends. Donald Trump tweeted the words 'Witch Hunt' more than three hundred times during his first presidency. While he uses the term to position himself as a perpetual victim, Fuentes takes a different and more direct approach when he speaks about bringing the witch hunts of the past back to control women and stop them from 'speaking in devilish tongues and casting spells' – i.e. speaking freely and exercising any degree of social power. The difference between Trump and Fuentes is that Nick is saying the quiet part out loud. When men talk about burning witches alive, what they are saying is that women need to be controlled. Women who cannot be controlled therefore need to be killed. This is why witches are casting hexes on figures like Fuentes and Trump.

In the lead-up to the 2016 US elections, a spell to bind Donald Trump went viral. Created and posted by Michael Hughes, thousands of witches both online and offline performed their own versions of the spell, adapting and improvising his original recipe. One of the key elements of this type of magical resistance I find particularly fascinating is the materiality of the rituals, the deliberately chosen artefacts and representations of things or people that they chose to incorporate into their spells. For example, the original spell calls for an 'unflattering photo of Trump' to link the spell to Trump and direct the energy of the spell towards him. Other iterations floating online showed people using other items to represent him, such as an orange candle, a carrot, or cheese puffs. The material 'stuff' of religion can offer a window into not only the types of beliefs in a religion or spiritual movement like witchcraft, but also the underlying ideologies that these beliefs rest upon.

Take, for instance, the use of orangey items in the Trump binding spell. On the one hand, these tell us that the rituals are drawing on a particular set of cosmological logics. Which tells us something about how witches see the world and all those, humans and nonhumans, that populate it as connected to one another via infinite and invisible threads. On the other hand, it tells us that witches have a wicked sense of humour. Using items that are orange is clearly meant to poke fun at Trump's fake tan. His orange glow has been a point of fascination and mockery for the internet for quite a while now. However, witches who deliberately used orange coloured items to represent him were not doing so simply to make fun of him. As early as 1968, anthropologist Mary Douglas talks about a kind of comedy that relies not on the humiliation of another person but on countering control with something uncontrollable and thus triumphing over it. She took this premise to formulate an understanding of humour as a social force that subversively challenges power. Humour and laughter can be powerful tools when it comes to social protest. As Douglas argues, comedy can be used to subversively challenge power. But what is it specifically that witches are challenging when they cast a hex on someone like Trump?

On the topic of magical resistance, anthropologist Sabina Magliocco writes that these forms of 'magical resistance emerged first from the religiously heterodox communities of modern Witches and Pagans, whose liberal, progressive, and universalist values were under direct assault by the president of the United States' (2020: 64). Similarly, the originator of the binding spell, Hughes (2018: 36), feared that he felt a 'creeping unease that Donald Trump's use of nationalism, xenophobia, racism, and misogyny during his campaign would lead him to victory'. Uneasiness, uncertainty and anxiety are emotions that have defined the past decade. Spells themselves, on a very simplistic level, could be seen as a tool for self-soothing during periods of social and political unrest. But I think this would be selling the potentiality and power of these types of rituals short. And also missing the broader historical and political context of these spells of resistance.

Too often, women's bodies are the subject of jokes, Trump's now famous pussy-grabbing crack being a prime (and hideous) example. This is why Radulescu (2012: 16) argues that, when it comes to 'female humour and creativity ... *mimicry and hysteria* [my emphasis] are dimensions of subversive forms of performance for women'. Sexist jokes are abundant, which is why the tables need to be turned. Put simply, to mock is to resist.

While these types of spells are forms of political protest, the fact that they went viral reveals their other critical role, as a social glue for people in times of division and uncertainty. Witchy author Pam Grossman (2019: 134), for example, writes about 'large public spells' like the one directed at Trump:

> I would offer that what public protest spells definitely do is build a sense of solidarity. Gathering in a group that has a shared goal reassures people that they are not alone, and that is consciousness-shifting in itself. Collective castings like these allow the disenfranchised to feel proactive and affirmed. They mobilize those who might otherwise be overwhelmed by despair, and they manifest catharsis and renewed strength. Group spells like these also put focus onto very real concerns about the dwindling safety of women, queer people, and people

of color. Whether this magic 'works' is subjective, it certainly amplifies the voice of resistance in its own cone of power.

I like how Grossman responds to the question 'Do these spells even work and if they don't what's the point?' with a resounding – *who cares?* Whether or not the spells 'work' is not the point. Focusing on the efficacy of a spell misses the point. It ignores the political power and potential of mass group spells. So they do work, in a sense, but socially – not magically.

A cause for castration

> Brock Allen Turner we hex you.
> You will be impotent
> You will know constant pain of pine needles in your guts
> Food will bring you no sustenance
> In water, your lungs will fail you
> Sleep will only bring nightmares
> Shame will be your mantle.
> You will meet justice.
> My witchcraft is strong. Our witchcraft is powerful. The spell will work. So Mote it be.[13]

This spell formed part of a hex circulated on Facebook in 2016 during the trial of Stanford University student Brock Turner. The hex was organized by Melanie Elizabeth Hexen, a midwife who lives near Wilton, Iowa. In an interview with *Vice* (Paul 2016) she explained that she and her local coven, made up of thirteen women, were inspired to create the event after feeling 'outraged and helpless' over Turner's short sentence.

Within twelve hours of the creation of the Facebook event to allow others who wanted to take action to join in on the

---

13 Melanie Elizabeth Hexen, Facebook post *circa* 2016.

mass hex, more than six hundred people had RSVP'd. Witches participated from various regions of the US as well as internationally, hexing in from countries such as Peru and Uruguay. Some women anointed their candles in urine or menstrual blood, and many incorporated sulphur or salt circles into their ritual. The witches deliberately layered forms of socially defined 'dirt' and filth like menstrual blood (just like the *Carrie* witch monster), and literal shit (one witch used their neighbour's dog's faecal matter) to drive home the message that Turner is a piece of (socially categorized) shit.

Hexen – great name for someone who organized a hex that went viral – said that many of the witches who participated were survivors of sexual assault themselves. They posted their own experiences in the Facebook event, sharing their support for one another. In her interview with *Vice*, Hexen expressed her deep gratitude for their involvement:

> I was touched so deeply they were involved in this ritual, and I feel that their witchcraft was ten times more powerful than mine in this situation. Someone who has been through something like that would have so much rage and so much power and so much need for justice that they made it so much stronger. It was brave of them to come forward and hopefully cathartic for them to do that.

I think the biggest difference between this ritual and the one cast on Trump is the intention. The spell on Trump was meant to bind him from doing harm to others, whereas the hex on Turner was designed to cause him harm. One line in particular caught my attention, which was the one that referred to making Turner 'impotent'.

Emasculation and castration: what a wicked combo. The hex invokes not only the fear of female castration, but the legacy and mythology tied up in the figure of the witch as one who disrupts the broader social order. It's a creative and deliberate play on some very old and tired sexist notions. But what is the exact nature of this social order that the witches are attempting to disrupt? Many witches claim it is patriarchy or sexism they are fighting, but how exactly are these terms defined or differentiated (if at all)?

In an interview with *Vox* (Illing 2020) Kate Manne explains that 'misogyny is not about male hostility or hatred toward women – instead, it's about controlling and punishing women who challenge male dominance'. Misogyny rewards women who reinforce the status quo and punishes those who don't. Sexism, on the other hand, is the 'ideology that supports patriarchal social relations, but misogyny enforces it when there's a threat of that system going away' (Illing 2020). Turner and Trump are a product of both sexism and misogyny.

Both Turner and Trump benefited from what Manne calls *himpathy*, which she defines as 'the disproportionate or inappropriate sympathy extended to a male perpetrator over his similarly, or less privileged, female targets in cases of sexual assault, harassment, and other misogynistic behaviour' (The Ethics Centre 2022). She gives the example of the treatment of Brett Kavanaugh during the Senate Judiciary Committee's investigation into allegations of sexual assault levelled against Kavanaugh by Professor Christine Blassey Ford. Manne points to the public's praise of Kavanaugh as a brilliant jurist who was being unfairly defamed by a woman who sought to derail his appointment to the Supreme Court of the United States as an example of himpathy in action. Kavanaugh, unsurprisingly, was also a target of mass hexes organized online. Himpathy operates in concert with misogyny. While misogyny seeks to discredit the testimony of women in cases of gendered violence, himpathy shields the perpetrators of that misogynistic behaviour from harm to their reputation by positioning them as 'good guys' who are the victims of 'witch hunts'.

Following his inauguration in 2017, Donald Trump tweeted the words 'Witch Hunt' roughly once every three days during his first presidency. A straightforward explanation for this behaviour is simple political distraction. But I think there was a more sinister and sophisticated reason behind this choice. By identifying himself as the victim of a witch hunt, Trump was able to condemn the charges against him as not only improbable, but impossible. Witch hunts are, by their very nature, illegitimate, their victims innocent, their judgements always wrong. Understandably, his use of this phrase has angered many witches. For example, Ann Hardman, a Louisville high priestess in the Fellowship of Isis, said that, 'it conjures up for me the burning of 10,000, mostly women, in England … who were accused as witches – right out of the Inquisition playbook' (Gerth 2018). This type of sentiment was commonly shared on social media and is drawn directly from Murray's theory of the witch-cult. These types of arguments against Trump using the 'witch hunt' either side-step or erase the witch hunts that are *currently happening* around the world today (Swanston and Gunga 2024; Raj 2023; Simoncelli and Lemmi 2020; Chaudhuri 2013). This erasure is deliberate and necessary for the narrative to retain its potency and political punch – that men like Trump and Kavanaugh and Turner are the victims of false accusations. Victims of cancel culture. Victims of hysterical mobs. *Victims.*

Online hexes attended by hundreds if not thousands of individuals are not simply a reaction to everyday misogyny and their intended targets. Fuentes, Trump, Turner and Kavanaugh are both symptoms and symbols of a broader society and culture so deeply steeped in sexism that it is practically invisible. Hexes that are held publicly are prime examples of digital feminist activism; they are designed to make sexism and misogyny visible.

A cyber coven

Giles: Are you a witch?
Jenny: I don't have that kind of power. 'Techno Pagan' is the term.
[Giles looks shocked]
Jenny: There are more of us than you think.[14]

We've come a long way since Jenny Calendar's proclamation as a 'techno-pagan' in this very early episode of *Buffy the Vampire Slayer* (*BTVS*). While various forms of media have played a significant role in exposing witchcraft beliefs and practices to a broader audience from television shows like *BTVS*, and from books and magazines, since the advent of the internet more and more practitioners are coming to the craft via social media. This growth has been well documented by sociologists Helen Berger and Douglas Ezzy in their book *Teenage Witches: Magical Youth and the Search for the Self* (2007), where they explore the beliefs and practices of young witches. Their study of almost one hundred young witches across America, England and Australia was one of the first to explore the ways the 'Internet [had come to be an] important form of mediated community for … young Witches' (2007: 43). When they were conducting their study, finding communities of interest online meant engaging in chat rooms. Since the good old 'chat room' days, a number of studies have been conducted on how witches use social media to connect with one another, to find information about the craft and to express their identity from Facebook (Renser and Tiidenberg 2020), to Instagram (Quilty 2022), to TikTok (Wiens and MacDonald 2024).

14 *Buffy the Vampire Slayer*: Season 1, episode 8 'I, Robot … You, Jane'.

Using such terms as 'techno pagan' or 'cyber coven' is more than a little outdated at this point in time. If I used them in a post they would be a dead giveaway that I'm an elder-millennial. Nowadays, witches are posting about swamp witches and vengeful sirens. One popular TikTok sound people are stitching is quite telling of the current mood: 'You may not be the girl of his dreams in the typical sense but you can always be the feral swamp witch that haunts his dreams and sends him increasingly disturbing visions until he comes crawling on his knees begging for mercy. Don't ever sell yourself short.' When I first heard this TikTok audio, I felt something stir inside me. It was something beyond hopefulness, it was a deep yearning for the world this TikTok gestures towards. Feminist media scholars Brianna Wiens and Shana MacDonald write about the rise of monstrous feminine figures like the witch (and the siren and the sea hag) within 'contemporary digital feminist and queer visual culture', arguing that these figures have 'found a prominent place within fourth wave digital feminist activism with practising witches attending key political moments in large numbers over the last decade' (2024: 73, 75). I would add to this that the mass online hexes organized over the past decade are a prime example of what Wiens and MacDonald call 'witchy feminist snaps' (2024: 76).

This idea is built on the concept of the 'feminist snap', which comes from feminist scholar Sara Ahmed. In *Living a Feminist Life* (2017), Ahmed describes the moment a twig snaps, seemingly sudden in its rupture, its breaking point. What is invisible is the pressure that slowly builds up before the twig breaks; a sudden event that is not so sudden. The hexes cast against Trump, Turner and Kavanaugh were not so sudden, even though they might have seemed so on the outside. These hexes were a 'witchy feminist snap', to borrow from Wiens and MacDonald (2024), but they were not the starting point, they were the start of something. The #MeToo movement was a collective and global feminist snap; it was 'more than a momentary eruption, but as a movement forward in the feminist struggle for justice and decency' (Jubas 2023: 143). The attraction of witchy symbols and rituals (such as hexes) reveals a significant shift towards a politics of refusal.

It's important to note that these hexes were not all met with welcome arms unanimously within the witchcraft communities. A private Facebook witchcraft group I'm part of recently posted a meme that captured some of the tensions that emerged around these spells. The image featured a figure standing in a field being shot with many arrows, each of which had words and phrases attached to them, like '3fold', 'karma', and 'love and light only'. Written above the figure and arrows is the text: 'Talking about hexes and curses in witchcraft groups.' The core sentiment being expressed here is that, for many of its practitioners, witchcraft is about spreading 'love and light only', and that its associated practices should work towards these goals only. The law of threefold being referenced here is the idea that for any kind of spell that is put out into the world, that same amount of energy will be returned three times over. It would follow, then, that a spell intended to cause harm, such as a hex, will result in a major backfire – i.e. have major negative consequences for the witch themselves.

The question of whether or not it is ethical to curse an individual (or even bind them from doing harm) has been the centre of a long-standing debate within the witchcraft community. As one Reddit user argued in a thread about the threefold law: 'You are not going to cast protection and undo the karmic entanglements or be able to protect yourself from consequences. There are many people that work hexes and negative Magick that have nothing (outwardly at least) bad happen to them.' While there were many who agreed with this sentiment and who joined in on mass hexes, there were many others who distanced themselves from the action and spoke out publicly against the spells. Reiki practitioner and tarot reader Staci Ivori (@stacivori on TikTok) suggests: 'Reclamation, self protection, and empowerment! Manipulation and ill intent for others becomes unnecessary when you focus on your own personal healing and evolutionary journey. More focus on you and yours than the worry of others' (cited in Stardust 2021). Others raised legitimate issues around organizing a mass spell with such a large number of practitioners. For example, whether posting the specifics of a hex to baby witches was wise when so many have not engaged in serious and prolonged reading, practice and training with an experienced mentor. Some did not believe that a public spell could be effective, arguing that magic was meant to be occult, practised in secret.

On the one hand, I thought it was very punk to organize a mass hex directed at individuals such as those I've discussed. It was political and funny and cathartic. In terms of my own practice and the type of hex I wanted to design, I knew that what I needed was something private.

There was something intimate about the whole situation, carving out a space and ritual to express the messy tangle of emotions I had been carrying around inside me. It would be nice if the five (or six or seven – however many) stages of grief unfolded in a nice linear fashion. Then it could be treated like a playbook to be followed, one transition ending cleanly before the next begins. In reality, it's more like being put through a washing machine that occasionally pauses long enough for you to realize you're in the machine before someone presses the button again and the emotions churn all over again. The idea of creating a hex seemed like the logical next step for me, to create a container for all the rage and grief I was feeling. So I set out to design a very special hex, a hex on my ex.

A hex on my ex

As a novice myself, not well versed in the left-hand path, I sought the advice of a witch I knew and trusted to tell about my desire to create a hex on my ex. I texted Fae: 'I need a hex, can you help me?'

I was surprised when she sent me a list of options rather than admonishing me for wanting to cast a hex in the first place. When I asked her why she didn't try to talk me out of it she said: 'So many people have asked me for spells and to be honest most of the time they chicken out. I think hexes and bindings have their place. You can't heal if you can't hex.'

For the spell, I had bought two human-shaped candles and some twine. I set the two figures on a dinner plate and twisted the twine around one figure, then looping it around the other. The figures and string were meant to symbolize our relationship, the emotional and energetic ties that were binding us together even after the separation.

As I read through Fae's instructions, I started to feel my nerves slip away. I was excited about the idea of taking action. Of *doing something*. I was ready to stop letting things happen, to do something over the top and a little dramatic. We don't often give ourselves the space to openly express emotions like rage and frustration. Nor do we have much in the way of ritual in our everyday lives – unlike my friend Fae, who weaves ceremony into every aspect of her life so it feels as natural as brushing one's teeth.

I struck the match and lit one end of the twine, closing my eyes and letting myself feel all the emotions I had been keeping at arm's length rise to the surface. Like bile in my throat. Something that is necessary in order to show up at work and be a functioning member of society. But the clawing, twisting tangle of feelings that lived in my chest needed somewhere to go, so into the jar they went. Squeezing my eyes shut, I let myself remember each and every insult. Every subtle put down. Every joke that barely concealed the intense cruelty and hatred he felt towards me. Feeling tears begin to flow, I also felt the hatred and shame I had been unknowingly directing towards myself. I thought about every time he would make fun of me, make me feel stupid. Every time he would subtly prevent me from seeing my family or friends. The guilt tripping. The messy web of love and loyalty and years together that kept me tethered to him, kept me from leaving him. I watched with a smile on my face as the threads slowly burned, turning black and, eventually, coming undone.

7

Reclaiming the Witch

Traditionally, tattoos have been used as rites of passage. In many societies, they signal the transition from adolescence to adulthood, or from one social status to another. They are an external manifestation of internal change and are revered as such. My tattoos signified a number of the transformations I had undergone throughout this chapter of my life, from leaving my toxic ex to rediscovering my witchy identity. More than a simple adornment, my tattoos are a physical archive, a living memory of my story. Who better to help me tell my story, than a wonderfully witchy tattoo artist?

Baba Vešterka, whose name means grandmother witch in Macedonian, lives and works in Melbourne, Australia. Baba operates out of The Scarlet Temple, a space that, like Baba themself, truly lives up to its name. As I ascend the stairs, I enter the deep red cave-like studio where I am faced with an altar with Medusa's head. Her effigy is surrounded by a beautiful yet chaotic array of artefacts, including a ferret pelt, skull candles, incense, a ouija board, dried flowers and ostrich feathers.

Baba is petite like myself, with dyed orange curls framing their face, the sides shaved and most of their hair pulled back into a ponytail. They wear a tight white t-shirt that reveals their extensively tattooed arms, the designs creeping up to their neck. Curling their legs up underneath them like a cat, they frown in concentration, putting some final details on the design they've created for my tattoo. Finally, they turned the iPad around to show me their work. I'm speechless at first. They have perfectly captured both the scene and the story and the feelings that I wanted this piece to express.

They place the stencil onto my upper arm and I gaze lovingly on the artistry in the mirror: a coven of witches fly high above the flames of a bonfire, no broomsticks required. Ascending into the sky, they twist and writhe together in the air. On the floor of the forest, two witches share a Sapphic embrace, almost devouring one another in their deep hunger for each other. Baba has created this design in their signature style, which was one of the key reasons I wanted them to be the one to create this piece. The way they create their witchy figures is using an etching style, making them look like they were created using a wood engraving print block. At first glance, they look like images one would expect to find in fifteenth- and sixteenth-century pamphlets disseminated to warn people of the dangers of witchcraft. Upon closer inspection, one discovers that the women are not portrayed in a way that is grotesque or comical; rather, they are exquisitely beautiful. Like many of Baba's other clients, we were all drawn to the figure of the witch because there is something powerful about embracing her and all her dark femininity. She might be damned, but she is free. To make her own choices. To carve out a new destiny.

Speaking of carving out, it was finally time for me to take my seat in the chair and let the process begin. Tattooing is quite a physically and emotionally demanding process and, as Baba explains to me, trauma that is stored in the body can resurface unexpectedly. About three or so hours into the process, my lower back was beginning to ache, and my fingers were tingly and numb from being outstretched for such a long time. I ask whether I was sitting still enough and, with a small smile, Baba told me I'm being perfectly still considering the quite painful area they are tattooing.

'Thank you', I said, 'I appreciate that. You know an ex-boyfriend of mine always told me I wouldn't be able to handle the pain of a tattoo. And because he has so many I just believed him.' Baba's face scrunches up in disgust: 'You are doing amazing, he couldn't have been more wrong.' I look down at their work and see the faces of the three witches look back at me. The feeling of getting this tattoo fills me with the same feeling of ecstatic freedom these witches embody as they levitate and dance amongst the trees and the stars. *Free at last.*

When I set out on this journey, what I wanted to understand is why people choose to call themselves witches. What does it mean to be a witch? What is the power in reclaiming this word, one that has such a long and painful legacy? Have they successfully reclaimed the 'witch' from its colonial and capitalist roots? Or is the project of reclamation, like the feminist project, always ongoing?

Under the guidance and teachings of the witches I have met along my journey, I began to understand how the figure of the witch was not simply a symbol of empowerment; she was something so much more than that. The witchy rituals I witnessed and participated in, from Red Tent gatherings, to worshipping Dionysus to getting a tattoo, were all sites of creativity and resistance. I came to realize that this creativity was not simply a practicality; rather, ritual creativity was providing these women with a safe space to reclaim their voices, their bodiliness, and to produce new ways of thinking.

Reclamation, resistance and refusal

The word 'reclaim' comes from the Latin *reclamare*, which means to 'cry out against'. To reclaim the witch means to cry out against sexism and misogyny. In Chapter 3, I discussed the ways in which witches attempt to reclaim their bodies from patriarchal discourses that anchor women's bodies in feelings of shame. The feminist project is one of reclamation. From reclaiming women in philosophy neglected by 'traditional' histories (Tyson 2014), to reclaiming the nipple or the tit (Thornton 2024), to reclaiming the witch. The tradition of witchcraft co-founded by Starhawk has reclamation embedded in both its very name and in its principles of unity. Starhawk writes:

> Our way out involves both resistance and renewal: saying no to what is, so that we can reshape and recreate the world. Our challenge is communal, but to face it we must be empowered as individuals and create structures of support and celebration that can teach us freedom. Creation is the ultimate resistance, the ultimate refusal to accept things as they are. (2009: 26)

Here, Starhawk invokes a hopeful vision for the future. One that requires both *resistance* and *refusal*. This vision of reshaping the world requires action at the level of both community and the individual, which necessitates support and constant care. How do we go about performing the levels of feminist care that this type of world building needs? In Chapter 2, I discussed both the potential of and the problems associated with how witchcraft uses 'self-care' in a way that individualizes, commodifies and depoliticizes what is, historically, a deeply radical feminist concept. Sara Ahmed shows how Audre Lorde makes it clear that 'caring for oneself is not about self-indulgence but self-preservation', it's about 'finding ways to exist in a world that makes it difficult to exist' (2017: 227). Radical self-care is both an act of resistance *and* a means of renewal. In this book, I have argued for more critical engagement with the types of 'self-care' that are used within some witchy groups and also products that are marketed to them.

Returning to Starhawk, her invitation for 'the way out' of the world in which we find ourselves is through resistance, which requires community. She defines what she means by this in *Dreaming the Dark* (1982: 122), where she explains that 'community means strength that joins our strength to do the work that needs to be done'. Her words remind me of bell hooks's discussion of beloved community, as something that 'is formed not by the eradication of difference but by its affirmation, by each of us claiming the identities and cultural legacies that shape who we are and how we live in the world' (1995: 265). In an interview, hooks discusses the necessity of *beloved community* in a world that operates on the politics and practices of domination (Brosi 2012). Domination, or 'power-over', as Starhawk (2009) would call it, requires constant and ever-evolving forms of resistance.

At first glance, domination and resistance seem to form quite a simple binary. Domination, within this binary framework, refers to institutionalized forms of power, which would mean that resistance is the organized opposition to power in a similarly institutionalized form. Political scientist and anthropologist James C. Scott (1987; 1992) invites us to pay attention to the pervasive and less organized, more everyday forms of resistance. One example he gives is gossip; he argues that, while gossip can be used by both the oppressed and oppressors, 'the power to gossip is more democratically distributed than power, property, and income, and, certainly, than the freedom to speak openly' (1992: 144). He continues: 'Witchcraft is in many respects the classical resort of vulnerable subordinate groups who have little or no safe, open opportunity to challenge a form of domination that angers them' (1992: 144).

In Chapter 5 I explored the idea of gossip as a practice of survival, as an everyday act of resistance to domination. The dismissal of gossip as idle women's words is, ironically, its power. The refusal to listen to gossip or to take those who engage in gossip seriously is what allows it to be disruptive. In this chapter, I also argue that the ridicule of women's words, being labelled as 'gossips' and accused of being witches, was also wrapped in the fear of covens being formed. Which, in essence, stems from a fear of women gathering, coalescing to gossip with one another. To complain. Maybe even to scheme and plot.

Circling back to the idea of beloved community, I draw on the work of Araby Smyth and colleagues (2020: 855) concerning the idea of forming *feminist covens* as 'momentary, inhabitable spaces where we dream of alternative futures and nurture our energies for revolutionary change' defined by 'willfulness to love and resist'. They call themselves a coven to 'conjur[e] the caring and threatening energy of witches' (Smyth et al. 2020: 856) and create these momentary spaces in the context of academia, a deeply hierarchical institution that holds a tremendous amount of power. Smyth and colleagues, like myself, are heavily influenced by Sara Ahmed's work and inspired by the figure of the feminist killjoy. Feminist covens are spaces for beloved community, to provide the strength and support to be able to 'do the work of being a wall, being a killjoy, being angry and unhappy' (Smyth et al. 2020: 855). Feminist covens are spaces of resistance.

It is from this position that I begin my list of witchy feminist resources, beginning with, unsurprisingly, the feminist covens. These resources are not exhaustive and I encourage you to create your own.

Covens

Where there is one witch, there will be others. Feminist covens are not restricted to academia or even to those practising witchcraft per se. They are spaces of resistance, refusal and, to Starhawk's point above, renewal. Feminism can be exhausting work; the work of being a witchy feminist is to refuse the ways of the world in order to imagine and hope for a better world. Feminist covens can provide spaces for renewal, a place for rest and reprieve. Somewhere to do the necessary care work when we are failed by the institutions or families we find ourselves in. A friend and colleague of mine, Esther Anderson (2019), reflected on an academic coven we formed while we completed our PhDs, a challenging time within a challenging environment. Although the members of our coven lived in different states, sometimes different countries altogether, we would still convene at yearly conferences, and gossip through a private Twitter group chat. Within our coven, we worked towards a 'cultivation of solidarity and care' (Anderson 2019) in a discipline that did not necessarily value or promote either of these behaviours. The decision to call ourselves a coven was made deliberately, because it 'implies both destabilization and reclamation of power, of feminist underpinnings' (Anderson 2019).

The term 'coven' shares the same etymological roots as the word 'convent', yet the two evoke very different images and feelings. One is made up of witches and the other of nuns. Strangely enough, both describe a collection of women, involved in spiritual endeavours and connected to one another through the bonds of sisterhood. These collective terms are both derived from the Middle English word *covin*, which means agreement.

Nuns have an agreement with God, a covenant if you will (another term with the same etymological genesis), through their vow of celibacy. They are essentially married to God. In the fifteenth to seventeenth centuries, similar phrasing was used to describe witches and their rituals – that, as part of their agreement with the devil, they were said to marry him. The devil, unlike God, was not satisfied with not being *ahem* satisfied. What this means is that, while nuns were expected to be virgins, witches were not. The pamphlets and books warning of the dangers of witchcraft were also filled with titillating accounts of witches' sexual acts with the devil.

This moral inversion was intentional and designed to create a sense of moral panic and fear towards witches, aka women. Feminist covens do not shy away from this history, but, rather, utilize the fear this term conjures up. In the words of the supreme witch of our time Cordelia Goode: *Satan has one son, but my sisters are legion motherfucker* (*AHS: Apocalypse*, Episode 10). I suggest that witchy feminists create covens, spaces of resistance, refusal and renewal. To do the work of being a wall, to lend each other the strength to resist and refuse. And, at the same time, to be a space for radical softness.

Books

A large part of the appeal of witchcraft stems from the idea that witches belong to a long lineage, a line that stretches back for generations often kept hidden for fear of persecution. As I have covered in Chapter 4, this myth of the matriarchal prehistory is just that, a myth. But there is power in feminist lineages. This book has guided you through my own feminist genealogy, one that is not necessarily linear, but a sprawling, complex web of theorists and activists who have shaped my thinking over the years. One of the most influential feminist thinkers for me has been Sara Ahmed, in particular her books *Living a Feminist Life* (2017) and *The Feminist Killjoy Handbook* (2023).

Other books on my witchy feminist resource list, ranging from academic to trade books to poetry, include: *Caliban and the Witch* (2004) and *Witches, Witch-Hunting, and Women* (2018), by Silvia Federici; *Down Girl: The Logic of Misogyny* (2017), by Kate Manne; *The Queer Art of Failure* (2011), by Jack Halberstam; *Witches, Sluts, Feminists* (2017), by Kristen Sollee; *In Defence of Witches: Why Women are Still on Trial* (2022), by Mona Chollet; *Witches, Feminism and the Fall of the West* (2021), by Marina Magloire; and *The Witch Doesn't Burn in This One* (2018), by Amanda Lovelace.

Altars

'A feminist life too is surrounded by things. Living a feminist life creates feminist things' (Ahmed 2017). I think about this quote by Sara Ahmed often, especially when I am writing and in the space I have created to do my thinking and reading and writing. I noticed that this is the place where I collect and use my 'feminist things', as Ahmed calls them; this is probably because this is where I spend most of my day. I noticed during my fieldwork that altars were commonplace in witches' homes, and at various points in my life I've had them in my house as well, depending on what I was going through at the time. Altars could also be created and packed back down for rituals held in public spaces, like parks or halls rented out. Altars are temporal, because they can be temporary. I even set up a temporary altar during a conference paper I delivered a few years back.

In Christianity, altars are used to sustain a system of meaning that values the masculine over the feminine. Altars are both a symbolic device designed to reify women's inferior status, and a 'social-structural arrangement that excludes women from the realm of religious and spiritual power' (Ortner 1974: 69). What altars symbolize is the materiality of spatial boundaries and gendered social structures. For example, in Christian settings, images of Jesus – statues, paintings and mosaics – are placed front and centre, commonly on or behind the altar. Altars generally sit within a broader masculine infrastructure of Christianity and are arguably an extension of this ideology. Witchy altars, by comparison, are an 'observable on-the-ground detail of women's activities often at variance with cultural ideology'

(Ortner 1974: 69). What this means, is that witchy altars are spaces for everyday resistance.

Altars are spaces for everyday resistance. I have argued elsewhere that altars are 'practice that helps ... young women to embed witchyness into the everyday' (Quilty 2020a: 107). I wish to build upon this idea, by proposing that altars can be spaces for witchy feminists to embed feminist ideas and practices into the everyday. Altars can also be spaces for resistance and renewal. On my altar (aka my desk) I keep a number of items, 'feminist things' as Ahmed calls them:

- Witchy artwork. During the infamous COVID lockdowns in Australia, many tattoo artists began selling prints to supplement their income while they could not see their clients. I became a fan of Baba Vešterka during this time, following them avidly on Instagram and I bought a series of their prints. These hang above my desk, watching over me as I write: witches and demon girls dancing around bonfires, sitting on top of piles of skulls surrounded by candles and pentagrams.
- A post-it note. When I feel overwhelmed with the state of the world, the violence in it, the sheer scope of suffering. I keep a list on this post-it note of things to do when the world rushes in and I can barely breathe: walk outside, breathe, play with my cats, call my sister. Not an earth-shattering list of new ideas, I know, but these are the things that work for me when I need to take care of myself so I can keep doing the work of reshaping the world.
- Postcards and letters. I have had many wonderful feminist and queer mentors over the years; their words in the form of postcards and letters are blue-tacked above my desk. Their words comfort and inspire me in equal measure.
- Feminist books (see above for my favourite feminist books).

Hexes

> You should be angry. You must not be bitter. Bitterness is like cancer. It eats upon the host. It doesn't do anything to the object of its displeasure. So use that anger. You write it. You paint it. You dance it. You march it. You vote it. You do everything about it. You talk it. Never stop talking it. (Angelou 2006)

In an interview, poet and civil rights activist Dr Maya Angelou discussed the importance of processing feelings like anger into art and into conversation. In the quote above, she affirms our feelings of rage and frustration – *You should be angry*. We have every right to be angry. Every morning the news brings more stories of women brutalized and raped. Trans women, Indigenous and Black women are being targeted and frustratingly underrepresented in the news. Stories about boyfriends, husbands, brothers and fathers enacting the worst kinds of violence on their girlfriends, wives, sisters and daughters. Every morning it makes me fucking angry. I keep Maya's words in my mind and in my heart when I read these stories. I have every right to be angry about living in a world where these things happen, where they are normalized and excused at every opportunity.

I also take to heart Angelou's call to *use that anger*. To write it, paint it, dance it, march it, vote for it and talk about it. To alchemize our anger. In Chapter 6, I gave examples of the mass online hexes that were performed in reaction to some of the most recognizable symbols of misogyny and sexism (in the West anyhow): Donald Trump, Brock Turner and Brett Kavanaugh. Hexes alchemize anger. Create your own hexes. Or draw on ones that already exist, for example, in books like Michael Hughes's *Magic for the Resistance* (2018). Starhawk has a brief guide to hexing on her official website.

In Chapter 6, I argued that this particular set of publicly performed hexes are a prime example of a witchy feminist snap that draws on a longer legacy of feminists using the witch and the fear she evokes. Here I am reminded of Sara Ahmed (2017), when she eloquently said 'it is dangerous to be perceived as dangerous'. Witchy feminists are dangerous. Hexes are a form of resistance and refusal, they are a mode of expressing a desire to reshape and recreate the world. In order to reshape the world, we need witchy feminists.

References

Aburrow, Y. (2009) Is It Meaningful to Speak of 'Queer Spirituality'? An Examination of Queer and LGBT Imagery and Themes in Contemporary Paganism and Christianity. In Hunt, S. (ed.), *Contemporary Christianity and LGBT Sexualities*. Ashgate.

Adler, M. (2006) [1979] *Drawing Down the Moon: Witches, Druids, Goddess-Worshippers, and Other Pagans in America Today*, rev. ed. Penguin Compass.

Ahmed, S. (2000) *Strange Encounters: Embodied Others in Post-Coloniality*. Routledge.

Ahmed, S. (2007) A Phenomenology of Whiteness. *Feminist Theory* 8 (2): 149–168.

Ahmed, S. (2010) *The Promise of Happiness*. Duke University Press.

Ahmed, S. (2017) *Living a Feminist Life*. Duke University Press.

Ahmed, S. (2023) *The Feminist Killjoy Handbook*. Penguin.

Aldred, L. (2000) Plastic Shamans and Astroturf Sun Dances: New Age Commercialization of Native American Spirituality. *American Indian Quarterly* 24 (3): 329–352.

Alvarado, D. (2020) *The Magic of Marie Laveau: Embracing

the Spiritual Legacy of the Voodoo Queen of New Orleans. Weiser Books.

Anderson, E. (2019) Making an Academic 'Coven'. *The Familiar Strange*, February 25.

Angelou, M. (2006) Maya Angelou, in conversation with Dave Chappelle. https://www.youtube.com/watch?v=okc6 COsgzoE.

Atwood, M. (1985) *The Handmaid's Tale*. HarperCollins.

Barney, S. A., Lewis, W. J., Beach, J. A. and Berghof, O. (2006) *The Etymologies of Isidore of Seville*. Cambridge University Press.

Barstow, A. (1994) *Witchcraze: A New History of the European Witch Hunts*. HarperCollins.

Berger, H. and Ezzy, D. (2007) *Teenage Witches: Magical Youth and the Search for the Self*. Rutgers University Press.

Boulware, J., Mathis, R., Yusef, K. and West-White, C. (2024) *Mamas, Martyrs, and Jezebels: Myths, Legends, and Other Lies You've Been Told about Black Women*. Black Lawrence Press.

Braakhuis, H. E. M. (2005) Xbalanque's Canoe. The Origin of Poison in Q'eqchi'-Mayan Hummingbird Myth. *Anthropos* 100 (1): 173–191.

Brooks, A. N. (2020) Fugitive Listening: Sounds from the Undercommons. *Theory, Culture and Society* 37: 25–45.

Brooks, K., Martin, K. and Simmons, L. (2021) Conjure Feminism: Toward a Genealogy. *Hypatia* 36: 452–461.

Brosi, G. (2012) The Beloved Community: A Conversation with bell hooks. *Appalachian Heritage* 40 (4): 76–86.

Bryant, K. (2017) Yes, Lana Del Rey Hexed Donald Trump. *Vanity Fair*, July 25. https://www.vanityfair.com/style/2017/07/lana-del-rey-spell-donald-trump.

Budapest, Z. (1980) *The Holy Book of Women's Mysteries: Feminist Witchcraft, Goddess Rituals, Spellcasting and Other Womanly Arts*. Wingbrow Press.

Califia, P. (1998) *Sensuous Magic: A Guide for Adventurous Lovers*. Masquerade Books.

California Native Plant Society (n.d.) Saging the World: Supporting Indigenous-led Efforts to Safeguard White Sage. https://www.cnps.org/conservation/white-sage.

Cannon, A. K. (2022) Plant of the Month: White Sage. https://daily.jstor.org/plant-of-the-month-white-sage/.

Castro, M. (2020) Introducing the Red Tent: A Discursive and Critically Hopeful Exploration of Women's Circles in a Neoliberal Postfeminist Context. *Sociological Research Online* 25 (3): 386–404.

Chagnon, C. W., Durante, F., Gills, B. K., Hagolani-Albov, S. E., ... Vuola, M. P. S. (2022) From Extractivism to Global Extractivism: The Evolution of an Organizing Concept. *Journal of Peasant Studies* 49 (4): 760–792.

Chaudhuri, S. (2013) *Witches, Tea Plantations, and Lives of Migrant Laborers in India: Tempest in a Teapot*. Lexington Books.

Chollet, M. (2022) *In Defence of Witches: Why Women are Still on Trial*. Picador.

Clark, E. S. (2020) Nineteenth-Century New Orleans Voudou: An American Religion. *American Religion* 2 (1): 131–155.

Clarke, A. (2001) *Tupperware: The Promise of Plastics in 1950s America*. Smithsonian Books.

Cloudcatcher WitchCamp (2024) https://www.cloudcatcherwitchcamp.com.au/.

Cohen, S. (1972) *Folk Devils and Moral Panics: The Creation of the Mods and Rockers*. Routledge.

Creed, B. (2023) *The Monstrous-Feminine: Film, Feminism, Psychoanalysis*, 2nd ed. Routledge.

Crenshaw, K. (1989) Demarginalizing the Intersection of Race and Sex: A Black Feminist Critique of Antidiscrimination Doctrine, Feminist Theory and Antiracist Politics. *University of Chicago Legal Forum* 1 (8): 139–167.

Crowley, V. (1996) *Wicca: The Old Religion in the New Millennium*. Thorsons.

Cusack, C. (2012) Charmed Circle: Stonehenge, Contemporary

Paganism, and Alternative Archaeology. *Numen* 59 (2–3): 138–155.

Cvetkovich, A. (2003) *An Archive of Feelings: Trauma, Sexuality, and Lesbian Public Cultures.* Duke University Press.

Daly, M. (1978) *Gyn/Ecology: The Metaethics of Radical Feminism.* Beacon Press.

Davies, O. (2007) *Popular Magic: Cunning-folk in English History.* Bloomsbury.

Deyrmenjian, M. (2020) Pope Innocent VIII (1484–1492) and the *Summis desiderantes affectibus. Malleus Maleficarum* 1. https://pdxscholar.library.pdx.edu/mmft_malleus/1/.

Diamant, A. (1997) *The Red Tent.* Allen & Unwin.

Douglas, M. (1966) *Purity and Danger: An Analysis of Concepts of Pollution and Taboo.* Taylor & Francis.

Douglas, M. (1968) The Social Control of Cognition: Some Factors in Joke Perception. *Man* 3 (3): 361–376.

Durkheim, É. (1915) [1912] *The Elementary Forms of the Religious Life*, trans. J. D. Swan. George Allen & Unwin.

Echols, A. (2019) [1989] *Daring to be Bad: Radical Feminism in America 1967–1975.* University of Minnesota Press.

Ehrenreich, B. and English, D. (2010) [1973] *Witches, Midwives, & Nurses: A History of Women Healers*, 2nd ed. The Feminist Press.

Eller, C. (1993) *Living in the Lap of the Goddess: The Feminist Spirituality Movement in America.* Beacon Press.

Eller, C. (2000) *The Myth of Matriarchal Prehistory: Why an Invented Past Won't Give Women a Future.* Beacon Press.

Ezzy, D. (2006) White Witches and Black Magic: Ethics and Consumerism in Contemporary Witchcraft. *Journal of Contemporary Religion* 21 (1): 15–31.

Ezzy, D. (2014) *Sex, Death and Witchcraft: A Contemporary Pagan Festival.* Bloomsbury.

Federici, S. (2004) *Caliban and the Witch: Women, the Body and Primitive Accumulation.* Autonomedia.

Federici, S. (2018) *Witches, Witch-Hunting, and Women*. Between the Lines Publishing.

Fludernik, M. (2017) Spectators, Ramblers and Idlers: The Conflicted Nature of Indolence and the 18th-Century Tradition of Idling. *Anglistik: International Journal of English Studies* 28 (1): 133–154.

Fobar, R. (2023) Somaliland's Frankincense Brings Gold to Companies. Its Women Pay the Price. *Guardian*, January 7. https://www.theguardian.com/world/2023/jan/07/somaliland-frankincense-female-workers-exploited-abuse.

Gardner, G. E. (1961) *Gardnerian Book of Shadows: The Complete Wicca Initiations and Pagan Ritual Lore*. Pantianos Classics.

Gerth, J. (2018) Louisville Witches are Vexed by Donald Trump's Talk of a 'Witch Hunt'. https://www.courier-journal.com/story/news/local/joseph-gerth/2018/12/18/louisville-witches-vexed-trumps-talk-witch-hunt/2347202002/.

Gibson, M. (2023) *Witchcraft: A History in Thirteen Trials*. Simon & Schuster.

Gill, T. M. (2010) *Beauty Shop Politics: African American Women's Activism in the Beauty Industry*. University of Illinois Press.

Goodwin, M. (2021) Witchcraft, White Feminism, and Intersectionality. https://medium.com/nuwitches/witchcraft-white-feminism-and-intersectionality-a9444a2dd1ec.

Greenwood, S. (2000) *Magic, Witchcraft and the Otherworld: An Anthropology*. Berg Publisher.

Grossman, P. (2019) *Waking the Witch: Reflections on Women, Magic, and Power*. Simon & Schuster.

Grosz, E. (1994) *Volatile Bodies: Towards a Corporeal Feminism*. Allen & Unwin.

Günel, G., Varma, S. and Watanabe, C. (2020) A Manifesto for Patchwork Ethnography. *Fieldsights*, June 9. https://culanth.org/fieldsights/a-manifesto-for-patchwork-ethnography.

Haight-Ashton, L. (2019) *Pagan Portals – The First Sisters: Lilith and Eve.* Moon Books.

Hage, G. (1998) *White Nation: Fantasies of White Supremacy in a Multicultural Society.* Routledge.

Halberstam, J. (2011) *The Queer Art of Failure.* Duke University Press.

Harrington, L. (2009) *Sacred Kink: The Eightfold Paths of BDSM and Beyond.* Mystic Productions Press.

hooks, b. (1995) *Killing Rage: Ending Racism.* Holt Paperbacks.

Horizon Institute (2020) Rape, Fornication and Other Related Offences Bill. (Law No. 78/2020). Republic of Somaliland. Unofficial English translation by Horizon Institute, 3 September. https://www.thehorizoninstitute.org/usr/documents/publications/document_url/33/horizon-institute-s-english-transation-of-the-bill-on-rape-fornication-and-other-related-offences-3-september-2020.pdf.

Howard, M. (2011) *Children of Cain: A Study of Modern Traditional Witches.* Three Hands Press.

Howes, H. E. (2024) *Poet, Mystic, Widow, Wife.* Bloomsbury.

Hughes, M. (2018) *Magic for the Resistance: Rituals and Spells for Change.* Llewellyn Publications.

Hume, L. (1997) *Witchcraft and Paganism in Australia.* Melbourne University Press.

Hurston, Z. N. (1938) *Tell My Horse: Voodoo and Life in Haiti and Jamaica.* Amistad Press.

Hutton, R. (1999) *The Triumph of the Moon.* Oxford University Press.

Hutton, R. (2017) *The Witch: A History of Fear, from Ancient Times to the Present.* Yale University Press.

Hutton, R. (2018) The Meaning of the Word 'Witch'. *Magic, Ritual and Witchcraft* 13 (1): 98–119.

Illing, S. (2020) What We Get Wrong About Misogyny. *Vox.* https://www.vox.com/identities/2017/12/5/16705284/elizabeth-warren-loss-2020-sexism-misogyny-kate-manne.

Ingold, T. (2008) When ANT Meets SPIDER: Social Theory for Arthropods. In Knappett, C., Malafouris, L. and Ingold, T. (eds.), *Material Agency*. Springer.

Javaid, A. (2020) Reconciling an Irreconcilable Past: Sexuality, Autoethnography, and Reflecting on the Stigmatization of the 'Unspoken'. *Sexualities* 23 (7): 1199–1227.

Jili, B. (2022) The Specter of Hobbes and Other White Men in African Anthropology. *Fieldsights*, April 14. https://culanth.org/fieldsights/the-specter-of-hobbes-and-other-white-men-in-african-anthropology.

Jubas, K. (2023) More Than a Confessional Mo(ve)ment? #MeToo's Pedagogical Tensions. *Adult Education Quarterly* 73 (2): 133–149.

Kaldera, R. (2006) *Dark Moon Rising: Pagan BDSM & the Ordeal Path*. Lulu.com.

Keene, A. (2018) Sephora's 'Starter Witch Kit' and Spiritual Theft. *Native Appropriations*. https://nativeappropriations.com/2018/09/sephoras-starter-witch-kit-and-spiritual-theft.html.

Kehoe, A. B. (2000) *Shamans and Religion: An Anthropological Exploration in Critical Thinking*. Waveland Press.

Kindig, J. (2018) All the Witches They Could Not Burn. *Boston Review*, December 4.

Kraemer, C. H. (2010) PantheaCon 2011 Report. *The Pomegranate: The International Journal of Pagan Studies* 12 (2): 276–280.

Kraemer, C. H. (2012) Gender and Sexuality in Contemporary Paganism. *Religion Compass* 6 (8): 390–401.

Kristeva, J. (1982) *Powers of Horror: An Essay on Abjection*. Columbia University Press.

Lau, K. (2000) *New Age Capitalism: Making Money East of Eden*. University of Pennsylvania Press.

Le Guin, U. K. (2016) *Words Are My Matter*. Small Beer Press.

Lepage, M. (2017) Queerness and transgender identity. *Studies in Religion* 46 (4): 601–619.

Levack, B. P. (2015) [1987] *The Witch-Hunt in Early Modern Europe*, 4th ed. Routledge.
Lorde, A. (1984) *Sister Outsider: Essays and Speeches*. Crossing Press.
Lorde, A. (1988) *A Burst of Light: Essays*. Firebrand Books.
Lorde, A. (2021) [1979] An Open Letter to Mary Daly. In Moraga, C. and Anzaldúa, G. (eds.), *This Bridge Called My Back. Writings by Radical Women of Color*, 40th anniversary ed. State University of New York Press.
Lovelace, A. (2018) *The Witch Doesn't Burn in This One*. Andrews McMeel Publishing.
Luhrmann, T. M. (1989) *Persuasions of the Witch's Craft: Ritual Magic in Contemporary England*. Harvard University Press.
Lutz, D. (2011) The Dead Still Among Us: Victorian Secular Relics, Hair Jewelry, and Death Culture. *Victorian Literature and Culture* 39: 127–142.
Mackay, C. S. and Institoris, H. (2009) *The Hammer of Witches: A Complete Translation of the Malleus Maleficarum*. Cambridge University Press.
Magliocco, S. (2020) Witchcraft as Political Resistance: Magical Responses to the 2016 Presidential Election in the United States. *Nova Religio: The Journal of Alternative and Emergent Religions* 23 (4): 43–68.
Magloire, M. (2023) *We Pursue Our Magic: A Spiritual History of Black Feminism*. University of North Carolina Press.
Manne, K. (2017) *Down Girl: The Logic of Misogyny*. Penguin Press.
Marantos, J. (2022) Smudge on an Ancient Practice: How to Help Stop the Poaching of the Region's Wild White Sage. *LA Times*.
McPhillips, K. (2000) Hidden Histories of the Menstrual Body. *Australian Religion Studies Review* 13 (2): 23–44.
McRobbie, A. and Garber, J. (2006) [1970] Girls and Subcultures. In Hall, S. and Jefferson, T. (eds.), *Resistance Through Rituals*, 2nd ed. Routledge.

Meredith, J. and Parma, G. (2018) *Elements of Magic: Reclaiming Earth, Air, Fire, Water & Spirit*. Llewellyn Publications.

Minh-Ha T. Pham (2017) Racial Plagiarism and Fashion. *QED: A Journal in GLBTQ Worldmaking* 4 (3): 67–80.

M. Macha NightMare and Vibra Willow (2002) *Origins of Reclaiming.* https://www.weaveandspin.org/reclaiming-history.

Morgain, R. (2010) *Beyond 'Individualism' Personhood and Transformation in the Reclaiming Pagan Community of San Francisco*. DPhil Thesis, Australian National University, Canberra.

Morgan, R. (2014) [1977] *Going Too Far: The Personal Chronicle of a Feminist*. Open Road Media.

Mueller, M. (2018) If All Acts of Love and Pleasure are Her Rituals, What About BDSM? Feminist Culture Wars in Contemporary Paganism. *Theology & Sexuality* 24 (1): 39–52.

Mukhtar, A. (2023) *Taliban Orders Afghanistan's Beauty Salons to Close in Latest Crackdown on Women's Rights*. https://www.cbsnews.com/news/taliban-afghanistan-beauty-salons-ordered-to-close-erasing-womens-rights.

Murib, Z. (2020) Backlash, Intersectionality, and Trumpism. *Signs: Journal of Women in Culture and Society* 45 (2): 295–302.

Murray, M. A. (1921) *The Witch-Cult in Western Europe: A Study in Anthropology*. Oxford University Press.

Murray, M. A. (1931) *The God of Witches*. Oxford University Press.

Neitz, M. J. (2000) Queering the Dragonfest: Changing Sexualities in a Post-Patriarchal Religion. *Sociology of Religion* 61 (4): 369–391.

Noble, C. (2005) From Fact to Fallacy: The Evolution of Margaret Alice Murray's Witch-Cult Theory. *The Pomegranate: The International Journal of Pagan Studies* 7 (1): 5–26.

Ortner, S. B. (1974) Is Female to Male as Nature is to Culture?

In Rosaldo, M. Z. and Lamphere, L. (eds.), *Woman, Culture, and Society*. Stanford University Press, pp. 68–87.

Oxford English Dictionary (2021) https://www.oed.com/discover/witch/?tl=true.

Paul, K. (2016) Hundreds of Witches Just Hexed Stanford Rapist Brock Turner. *Vice*, June 9.

Penny, L. (2014) *Unspeakable Things: Sex, Lies and Revolution*. Bloomsbury.

Poutiainen, E. (2023) A Feminism of the Soul? Postfeminism, Postsecular Feminism and Contemporary Feminine Spiritualities. *European Journal of Cultural Studies* 27 (6): 1–18.

Queer Healing Journeys (2019) Race & Appropriation in Pagan Community with Gede Parma. https://queerhealingjourneys.com/gede-parma/.

Quilty, E. (2020a) Everyday Witches: Identity and Community among Young Australian Women Practising Witchcraft. PhD Thesis, University of Newcastle, Australia.

Quilty, E. (2020b) Letting the Juices Flow: Reclaiming the Body Through Witchcraft. In Page, S. and Pilcher, K. (eds.), *Embodying Religion, Gender and Sexuality*. Routledge.

Quilty, E. (2022) #Witchlife: Witchy Digital Spaces. *Journal of Contemporary Religion* 37 (1): 29–49.

Radulescu, D. (2012) *Women's Comedic Art as Social Revolution*. McFarland & Company.

Raj, S. (2023) India Struggles to Eradicate an Old Scourge: Witch Hunting. *New York Times*, May 13.

Reclaiming Collective (2021) Principles of Unity. https://reclaimingcollective.wordpress.com/principles-of-unity/.

Renser, B. and Tiidenberg, K. (2020) Witches on Facebook: Mediatization of Neo-Paganism. *Social Media + Society*: 1–11.

Rhodes, J. (1990) Marie Laveau, Voodoo Queen. *Feminist Studies* 16 (2): 331–344.

Richmond, K. (2012) Through the Witch's Looking Glass: The Magick of Aleister Crowley and the Witchcraft of Rosaleen

Norton. In Bogdan, H. and Starr, M. P. (eds.), *Aleister Crowley and Western Esotericism*. Oxford University Press.

Rountree, K. (2003) *Embracing the Witch and the Goddess: Feminist Ritual-Makers in New Zealand*. Routledge.

Said, E. (1978) *Orientalism*. Pantheon Books.

Salomonsen, J. (2002) *Enchanted Feminism: The Reclaiming Witches of San Francisco*. Routledge.

Sayer, D. (2009) Curses and Hexes. In Bryant, C. D. and Peck, D. L. (eds.), *Encyclopedia of Death and the Human Experience*. SAGE Publications.

Scott, J. C. (1987) *Weapons of the Weak: Everyday Forms of Peasant Resistance*. Yale University Press.

Scott, J. C. (1992) *Domination and the Arts of Resistance: Hidden Transcripts*. Yale University Press.

Sheppard, K. L. (2013) [1976] *The Life of Margaret Alice Murray: A Woman's Work in Archaeology*. Lexington Books.

Simoncelli, M. and Lemmi, D. (2020) *In Pictures: The Witch Hunts of Bangui*. Al Jazeera, March 24. https://www.aljazeera.com/gallery/2020/3/24/in-pictures-the-witch-hunts-of-bangui.

Smith, M. (2002) The Flying Phallus and the Laughing Inquisitor: Penis Theft in the 'Malleus Maleficarum.' *Journal of Folklore Research* 39 (1): 85–117.

Smyth, A., Linz, J. and Hudson, L. (2020) A Feminist Coven in the University. *Gender, Place & Culture* 27 (6): 854–880.

Sollee, K. J. (2017) *Witches, Sluts, Feminists: Conjuring the Sex Positive*. ThreeL Media.

Spivak, G. C. (1994) Can the Subaltern Speak? In Williams, P. and Chrisman, L. (eds.), *Colonial Discourse and Post-Colonial Theory: A Reader*. Routledge.

Stardust, L. (2021) Witches Hex Trump and His Supporters After Capitol Insurrection. *Teen Vogue*, January 12.

Stardust, Z. (2024) *Indie Porn: Revolution, Regulation, and Resistance*. Duke University Press.

Starhawk (1979) *The Spiral Dance: A Rebirth of the Ancient Religion of the Great Goddess*. Harper.

Starhawk (1982) *Dreaming the Dark: Magic, Sex and Politics*. Beacon Press.

Starhawk (2009) [1990] *Truth or Dare: Encounters with Power, Authority, and Mystery*. HarperCollins.

Stone, M. (1976) *When God Was a Woman*. HMH Books.

Summers, A. (2016) [1975] *Damned Whores and God's Police*. NewSouth Publishing.

Summers, M. (2011) *A Popular History of Witchcraft*. Routledge.

Swanston, T. and Gunga, T. (2024) Claims of Witchcraft Can Lead to Murder. ABC news. https://www.abc.net.au/news/2024-04-13/claims-of-witchcraft-can-lead-to-murder-in-png/103682576.

The Ethics Centre (2022) Big Thinker: Kate Manne. https://ethics.org.au/big-thinker-kate-manne/.

Thompson, S. (2011) An Open Letter to All Pagans, and Particularly the Pantheacon Organizers (Pantheacon 2011). https://st4r.org/an-open-letter-to-all-pagans-and-particularly-the-pantheacon-organizers-pantheacon-2011/.

Thompson, S., Pond, G., Tanner, P., Omphalos, C. and Polanshek, J. (2012) *Gender and Transgender in Modern Paganism*. Lulu.com.

Thornton, S. (2024) *Tits Up: What Our Beliefs about Breasts Reveal about Life, Love, Sex and Society*. Pan Macmillan.

Turner, V. (1969) *The Ritual Process: Structure and Anti-Structure*. Aldine de Gruyter.

Tyson, S. (2014) From the Exclusion of Women to the Transformation of Philosophy: Reclamation and its Possibilities. *Metaphilosophy* 45 (1): 1–19.

Ward, M. (2004) *Voodoo Queen: The Spirited Lives of Marie Laveau*. University Press of Mississippi.

Weiss, M. (2011) *Techniques of Pleasure: BDSM and the Circuits of Sexuality*. Duke University Press.

White, E. D. (2018) The Creation of 'Traditional Witchcraft': Pagans, Luciferians, and the Quest for Esoteric Legitimacy. *Aries* 18 (2): 188–216.

Wiens, B. I. and MacDonald, S. (2024) Witches in Swamps, Sirens at Sea, Leviathans of the Deep: Feminist Figures that Haunt our Social Media World. University of Waterloo, Preprint. http://hdl.handle.net/10012/20387.

Wolfe, P. (1998) *Settler Colonialism and the Transformation of Anthropology: The Politics and Poetics of an Ethnographic Event*. Cassell.

Index

Note: Page numbers followed by "n" refer to endnotes.

#MeToo movement, 3, 15, 149–150
2011 Pantheacon, 104–106

abjection theory, 139, 140
abstinence-based sex education, 75
Aburrow, 104
Adler, M., 8, 9
Ahmed, S., 55, 149, 157, 159, 161–162, 164
Alder, M., 12
Aldred, L., 55
altars, 162–163
Amazon Priestess Tribe, 104
American Voodoo, founder and priestess of, 111
ancestors, rituals for, 114–115, 118
Anderson, E., 160
Angelou, M., 164
anger, 128, 164
Anthony, S. B., 8, 27–28
anthropology, studying witchcraft in, 12
anxiety, 80, 143
Asli Maydi company, 46

Atlantic slave trade, 111
Atwood, M., 1–2
Australian context, witchcraft in, 28–30
Australian Reclaiming community, 20
authentic self, 57
autoethnography, 13–15

babalawo (diviner or priest), 119
Baba Vešterka, 154–156, 163
'the bad witch', 138
Barstow, A., 138
BDSM and kinky techniques, 17, 66, 68–69
beauty salons role in civil rights activism, 124
bedknobs, 77–79
'bedroom culture', 77
beloved community, 158–159
beloved dead, 118
Berger, H., 148
biohacking, 43
biological essentialism, 58–59, 103

Index

black markets, 52–55
black witch, 55
black witchcraft, 138
Black women
   and black beauty industry, 124
   and Jezebel myth, 79
   underrepresentation in news, 164
   as Voodoo villains, 113
   writing practices, 114
blood magic, 40–44, 57
Bon, D., 140
books as witchcraft resources, 161–162
bower, 64–65, 67–68
Brooks, A. N., 124
Brooks, K., 114
broomsticks, 77–79
Budapest, Z., 8, 10, 27
Buffy the Vampire Slayer (*BTVS*) (movie), 77, 83, 137, 148

Calendar, J., 148
Caliban and the Witch (Federici), 80, 161
Califia, P., 69
Camille (Voodoo priestess), 109–110, 113, 116, 131
   House of Voodoo, 121–122
   practises, 110
   Victorian practice of hair art, 121
Cannon, A. K., 54
capitalism, 26, 128
   Church and early stages of, 81
   exploitative relations of, 81
   New Age, 47, 53, 55–56
Carrie (movie), 139
casting circle, practice of, 34–37
castration
   cause for, 144–147
   fear of female castration, 139, 145–146
Castro, M., 49
Catholicism, 32, 33, 82, 89, 116, 119
Celtic gods, 98

Celtic paganism, 33
Chagnon, C., 56
Charmed (movie), 77, 83, 137
Chollet, M., 161
Christian cosmology, 78
Christianity, 99–100
Chumash, T. L. L., 54
The Clan of Tubal Cain, 88–89
Clarke, A., 48
CloudCatcher witchcamps, 20, 88, 104
   Elements of Magic Path, 22–25
   in Springbrook National Park, 19–22
   unbelonging, 30–34
Cochrane, R., 88–89, 97–98
Code Noir, 124, 124n12
Cohen, S., 6
colonialism, 26, 55
   common tactic of settler, 52
   covens, conspiracies and, 126–129
colonialism and capitalism and Christianity (big three C's), 102
colonial violence, 27, 130
community, 158
   Australian Reclaiming, 20
   beloved, 158–159
   multicultural, 29
   queer community archives, 105–106
conjure feminism, 114
conspiracies
   covens, colonialism and, 126–129
   from hell, 134–136
constant labour, necessity of, 128
contemporary spirituality, 82–83
contemporary witchcraft, 7, 10, 12, 16, 45, 81, 101, 103
cosmological logics, 142
covens
   of witches, 126–129, 135, 159–161
   women-only, 10

The Craft (movie), 77–78
Creed, B., 139–140
Crenshaw, K., 27
creolization, 119
Crowley, A., 7, 42
Crowley, V., 36
Crow Ritual, 105–106
Crucifixion, 126
'cultivation of solidarity and care', 160
cultural appropriation, 31, 37, 56
'culture wars', 27
curses, 136–137. *see also* hex(es)
  ethics in, 150
  fear of female castration, 139–140
  menstruation, 139–140
  and witchcraft practices, 138
Cvetkovich, A., 106
Cybele (ancient Greek god), 35
cyber coven, 148–151

Daly, M., 28
Damh the Bard (musician), 98
Damned Whores and God's Police (Summers), 75
dark moon rituals, 59
'Dead Men Don't Rape' (song by Delilah Bon), 140
Death Witch, 109
  conjure feminism, 114
  covens, conspiracies and colonialism, 126–129
  hair, grief and gossip, 120–126
  love, longing and loas, 118–120
  rituals, 114–118
  visiting Marie's tomb, 129–132
determinism, belief in, 92
Diamant, A., 39
Dianic witchcraft, 27
digital feminist activism, 147
domestic life structures, 10
domination, 26, 27, 158
doTERRA, 45–48
Douglas, M., 62, 142

Down Girl: The Logic of Misogyny (Manne), 16, 161
Drawing Down the Moon: Witches, Druids, Goddess-Worshippers, and Other Pagans in America Today (Adler), 8–9
Dreaming the Dark, 158
Druidry, 100
Durkheim, É., 23
Dutton, E., 161

Early Modern Christendom, witch trials of, 99
Earthsong camp, 20, 25
eclecticism, 56
eclectic spiritual extractivism, 55–59
economic enclosure process, 124
Ehrenreich, B., 6, 101–102
Elements of Magic: Reclaiming Earth, Air, Fire, Water & Spirit (Meredith and Parma), 23, 24
Elements of Magic Path, 22–25
  casting circle practice, 34–37
  community-building capacity of ritual, 23–24
  spiral dance from evening ritual, 24
  weaving, 23–25
Eller, C., 101, 136
emasculation, 145–146
English, D., 6, 101–102
entertainment, 125
ethnography, 13–14
European folklore, 94
exotic Eastern religions, 58
extractivism, eclectic spiritual, 55–59
Ezzy, D., 42, 148

fairy circles, 94
  European folklore as, 94–95
  liminal space, 94, 97
  witchcraft rituals, 95

fate, threads of, 89, 92
fear(s)
    of covens of witches, 128, 159
    of death, 115
    of female castration, 139, 145–146
    liminal and, 94
    menstruation and, 61–62, 107
    of scary movies, 137
    of witches, 80, 161
    about women and social power, 125–127
Federal Reserve Treasury Bank, 135
Federici, S., 5–6, 80, 126, 138, 161
female castration, fear of, 139, 145–146
feminist/feminine/feminism, 26, 134, 136, 159–160
    books, 163
    covens, 159, 161
    first wave, 6
    snap, 149
    spiritualties, 58
    things, 162
    witchy/witches, 7–11, 15–18
The Feminist Killjoy Handbook (Ahmed), 161
first wave feminism, 6
Fludernik, M., 128
folk songs, 98
fondness, 84
Ford, C. B., 146
Fortune, D., 7
French Catholicism, 119
fringe archaeology. *see* pseudo-archaeology
Fuentes, N., 133, 140–141

Garber, J., 77
Gardner, G., 7, 97–98
gender binary of male/female and god/goddess, 103
gendered violence, 134, 146
gender essentialism, 10, 11
Gill, T., 124

Gina, 112–113, 116, 120, 131
god-worship, 88
Goddess movement, 100
god/goddess, gender binary of, 103
The God of Witches (Murray), 7
godparent, 125
Going Too Far: The Personal Chronicle of a Feminis (Morgan), 135
Gondwana Rainforests, 19
Goode, C., 161
Goodwin, M., 27
Goop website, 53
gossip, 120–126, 158–159
gossip's bridle. *see* scold's bridle
Greenwood, S., 36, 59
grief, 120–126
Grossman, P., 143–144
Grosz, E., 61
group spells, 143–144
Gyn/Ecology (Daly), 28

Hage, Ghassan, 29
Haight-Ashton, L., 104
hair, 90, 120–126
    hair-braiding, 122
    hairwork, 121–122
    Victorian practice of hair art, 121
Halberstam, J., 14, 161
Half-Hanged Mary (Atwood), 1–2
The Hammer of Witches (Mackay and Institoris), 5
The Handmaid's Tale (Atwood), 1, 2
Hardman, A., 147
Harrington, L., 69
harrowing, 94
Hekate (ancient Greek goddess), 89
hex(es), 133–134, 136–140, 151–153, 164–165. *see also* curses
Hexen, M. E., 144
high theory, 14
himpathy, 146
Hinduism, 32–33
    feeding ancestors in, 115

mundan (hair-shaving ceremony) in, 90
wellness in, 58
Hocus Pocus (movie), 3
The Holy Book of Women's Mysteries (Budapest), 8
hooks, b., 158
'House of Voodoo', 13, 121
Howes, H. E., 126
Hughes, M. M., 134, 141, 143, 164
human potential movement, 36
Hume, L., 12, 36, 95
humour sense, 126, 142
hunger, 67, 155
Hutton, R., 7

idle talk, 127
In Defence of Witches: Why Women are Still on Trial (Chollet), 161
Indigenous women, underrepresention in news, 164
Ingold, T., 92
intersectionality, 27–28
Ivori, S., 150–151

Javaid, A., 15
Jezebel myth, 79
Jim Crow-era laws, 111
junk archaeology. *see* pseudo-archaeology

Kaldera, R., 69
Kavanaugh, B., 18, 134, 146, 147, 149, 164
Keene, A., 54
Kehoe, A. B., 53
Kindig, J., 80
Kraemer, C. H., 10, 103
Kramer, H., 5, 138
Kristeva, J., 139

'large public spells', 143
LARPing, 44

Lau, K., 47
Lavallee, R., 30
Laveau, M., 109, 111–112, 118
as hairdresser, 123
location of tomb, 116
social power, 123–124
visiting to tomb of, 129–132
Le Guin, U. K., 102
letters of feminist and queer mentors, 163
'light and love', 138
liminal, 94–95, 97, 132
liminal period, 95
Living a Feminist Life (Ahmed), 149, 161
loas in New Orleans Voodoo, 110, 118–120
longing, 118–120
Lorde, A., 28, 50, 157
love, 118–120
Lovelace, A., 162
low theory, 14
Luhrmann, T., 10

Macdonald, S., 149
magical resistance, 140–143
Magic for the Resistance (Hughes), 164
Magliocco, S., 142
Magloire, M., 112, 162
male/female, gender binary of, 103
Malleus Maleficarum (Kramer), 5, 80, 138
Manne, K., 16, 146, 161
Martin, K., 114
mass hexes, 18, 146, 149–151, 164
materiality of rituals, 141–142
matriarchal myth, 101
matriarchal prehistory
Murray's theory of, 100
myth of, 136
matriarchal utopia, 97
Mayan mythology about menstruation, 42

Index

McRobbie, A., 77
menstrual/menstruation, 41
   blood rituals. *see* blood magic
   and fear(s), 61–62, 107
   magic. *see* blood magic
   Mayan mythology about, 42
   taboos, 41, 43, 44, 107
Meredith, J., 23, 24
Methodism, 89
Midler, B., 3
midlife crisis, 93
mighty dead, 118–119, 131
Minh-Ha T. Pham, 56
misogyny, 3, 16, 133, 146
modern witchcraft, 10
monstrous-feminine, 139, 140
moral panic, 6
Morgan, R., 98, 135
Mueller, M., 68
multicultural community, 29
The Mummy (movie), 137
mundan (hair-shaving ceremony), 90
Murray, M. A., 6–7, 98–100

natural catastrophes, 41
nature witch
   CloudCatcher witchcamps, 88
   cult of women, 100–106
   fairy circles, 94–97
   Methodism, 89
   temples, tents and taboo, 106–108
   war on witches, 97–100
   weaving magic, 90–94
New Age
   capitalism, 47, 53
   movement, 36
   spirituality, 45, 138
   Tupperware parties, 44–49
NightMare, M. M., 9
Nixon, R., 135
Noah's Ark, 126
nuns, 160

olúwa (god), 119
online hexes, 147, 149, 164
Open Source Alexandrian Witchcraft Tradition website, 105
oppression, 120
   cycles of, 101–102
   Lilith's story of, 104
   resistance of, 140
   seeing all systems of, 26, 27
oriental 'Other', 79
Origins of Reclaiming (NightMare and Willow), 9
Orion, L., 12

paganism, 10–11, 33
pagans, 57, 106, 142
   conversion to Christianity, 33
   in North America, 104
   'Pagans in the Pub' monthly events, 12
Papal Bull of Innocent VIII, 99
Parker, S. J., 3
Parma, G., 23
patriarchy, 88, 135–136, 139
period taboos, 40–41
plastic shamans, 55
plays, 125–127
political hexes, 134
postcards of feminist and queer mentors, 163
post-it note, 163
power
   power-over, 26, 158
   power-with, 26
   power-within, 26
   of witchcraft, 138
   witches, women and, 4–7
Practical Magic (movie), 77, 137
primitive accumulation, 81
Principles of Unity, 26–27
pseudo-archaeology, 100
public hexes, 134, 165
public protest spells, 143
public spell, 151

Index

The Queer Art of Failure (Halberstam), 161
queer community archives, 105–106
queer resistance, 104

racial/race
  issue in witchcraft, 29–30
  logics, 55
  plagiarism, 56–57
  politics and Reclaiming witchcraft, 25–29
radical abjection, 140
radical political feminism, 50
radical self-care, 157
Ramirez, R., 53
Reclaiming witchcamp, 19, 69
reclaiming witchcraft. *see also* Starhawk
  in Australian context, 28–30
  racial politics and, 25–28
  Sacred Kink and tradition, 67–70
Rede, W., 92
Red Tent discourse, 107
red tent gatherings, 17, 39–40, 43, 44, 46–49, 51, 55, 57–59, 61–62
The Red Tent (Diamant), 39–40
refusal, 157–159, 161, 165
reincorporation, 95
resistance, 157–159
Rey, L. D., 134
'Rite of Lilith', 104
ritual(s), 10, 16, 17, 60, 142
  artefacts, 90, 141
  of burning white sage, 52
  casting circle, 34–37
  in CloudCatcher witchcamp, 20
  creativity, 156
  Crow Ritual, 105, 106
  dark moon, 60
  devotional, 104
  of discipline, 123
  feeding ancestors, 114–116
  fertility, 84
  hair use in, 90

magic and, 42, 84
menstrual blood, 57, 62, 145
menstruation, 40, 61
Rountree's argument, 23–24
Voodoo, 90
in Wild Maine camp, 26
witchcraft, 95–96, 103
Rountree, K., 11, 23

Sacred Kink' workshop, 17, 66–70, 85
Sacred Round on Stolen Ground: Decolonizing your Magical Practice, A (Lavallee), 30
sage smudge stick, 51–53
scold's bridle, 127, 128
Scott, J. C., 158
second wave feminism, 6n2, 9–10, 101
self-care, 157
  radical, 157
  spiritual self-improvement and, 49–51
self-help pop psychology, 55
separation, 36, 95, 152
Sephora, 53
settler colonialism, 52–55
Settler Colonialism and the Transformation of Anthropology (Wolfe), 29
sex(ism)/sexuality, 2, 3, 16, 69–70, 79, 146
  education, 67, 75–76
  sexist jokes, 143
  sexual assault allegations, 146
  sexual politics of Reclaiming witchcraft, 68
  type describing by Starhawk, 70
sex witch
  bedknobs and broomsticks, 77–79
  bower, 64–65
  Church of Wicca, 81–86
  God's police and damned witches, 74–76

sex witch (*cont.*)
    homecoming from witchcamp, 70–74
    Sacred Kink and Reclaiming Witchcraft tradition, 67–70
    saving women from sexual nature, 79–81
    shame, 17, 31, 43, 45, 79, 92, 106, 152, 157
Simmons, L., 114
sin, 75, 127
sinfulness of idleness, 128
Skeleton Key (movie), 113
Small, D., 53
smudging, 52–53, 55, 56
Smyth, A., 159
social
    control, 120
    order, 14, 16, 41, 43, 111, 126, 138, 139, 145–146
    power, 27, 123–125, 141
    taboos, 41, 107
socialization, 85
social taboos, 107–108
Sollée, K., 5, 161
spatiality of cemeteries, 131
spells, 30, 46, 76, 97, 150, 152. *see also* curses; hex(es)
    binding, 133, 134, 142, 143
    love, 112
    public, 143–144, 151
    of resistance, 143
'Spell to Bind Donald Trump and All Those Who Abet Him, A', 134, 141
The Spiral Dance: A Rebirth of the Ancient Religion of the Great Goddess (Starhawk), 8
spirit(s), 23, 112, 116–117, 119
The Spirit of Albion (short film), 98
spiritual practices, 44–45
    commodification, 40
    eclectic, 49

spiritual/spirituality/spiritualism, 49–50, 82, 122
    eclectic spiritual extractivism, 55–59
    New Age, 45, 138
    self-improvement, 49–51
    wellness, 47, 57
    women, 10, 58
Springbrook National Park, 19–22
Starhawk (American author), 8, 164
    definition of power, 26–27
    about feminist covens, 159–160
    about importance of community, 157–158
    about 'matriarchal utopia' destruction, 97–98
    about misogyny, 79–80
    Reclaiming witchcraft tradition, 10, 24, 157
    and red tent gatherings, 59
    about sex, 69–70
Stonehenge, 100
Stone, M., 100
Summers, A., 75
super sexy (Parker), 3

taboo(s) 40, 106, 118
    menstrual, 41, 43, 44, 107
    period, 40–41
    social, 41, 107–108
tattooing/tattoos, 154, 155
techno-pagan, 148–149
techno witch, 133
    castration, cause for, 144–147
    conspiracy from hell, 134–136
    cosmological logics, 142
    curses and white magic, 136–140
    cyber coven, 148–151
    hexes, 133–134, 136–140, 151–153
    magical resistance, 142–143
    materiality of rituals, 141–142
    oppression and control, 140
    spells, 143–144

Index

Teenage Witches: Magical Youth and the Search for the Self (Berger and Ezzy), 148
Temperance, 65, 81–85
temples, 106–108
tents, 106–108
Thompson, S., 105
Tiff, 65, 74–75, 78, 82
torture, 73, 127, 137
transgender individuals
  exclusion of, 59, 103
  presence at events and festivals, 103–104
Trans women, underrepresentation in news, 164
Trump, D., 141–143, 146–147, 149, 164
Turner, B., 134, 144, 146–147, 149, 164
Turner, V., 95

unbelonging, 30–34
uncertainty, 143
uncivilized savages, 79
uneasiness, 143

Vice magazine, 52, 144–145
virtuous wives, 75–76
Voodoo in New Orleans, 13–14. *see also* Laveau, M.
  ancestral worship in, 118–120
  characterization, 111
  conceptualization of death, 115–116
  conjure feminism, 113–114
  dolls, 90
  hair use in rituals, 90
  illegality of, 110–111
  priestess/women in, 110, 112–113, 129
  rejecting linearity of time, 116
  research in, 129–130
Vox magazine, 146

weaving magic, 24–25, 90

ant and spider conversation, 92–93
harrowing, 94
incongruous beliefs, 92
midlife crisis, 93
ritual artefacts, 90
white magic, 42, 136–140
Webster, M., 1, 4
Weiss, M., 69
wellness brands, 47, 49
We Pursue Our Magic: A Spiritual History of Black Feminism (Magloire), 161–162
When God Was a Woman (Stone), 100
white magic, 42, 136–140
white multiculturalism, 29
white sage, 52–55
white witch, 55
  blood magic, 40–44
  dark thoughts during new moon, 59–63
  eclectic spiritual extractivism, 55–59
  New Age Tupperware parties, 44–49
  The Red Tent, 39–40
  spiritual self-improvement and self-care, 49–51
  white sage, black markets and settler colonialism, 52–55
white witchcraft, 42–43, 138
Wicaan rituals, 10
Wicca, Church of, 81–86
Wiens, B., 149
Wildkin camp, 20, 25
Wild Maine camp, 26
Willow, V., 9, 38–39, 44–51, 57, 59–60, 62, 83, 103, 107
The Witch-Cult in Western Europe (Murray), 99
witchcamps, 25, 67. *see also* CloudCatcher witchcamps
  Earthsong camp, 20, 25

witchcamps (*cont.*)
  homecoming from witchcamp, 70–74
  Reclaiming witchcamp, 19, 69
  Wildkin camp, 20, 25
  Wild Maine camp, 26
witchcraft, 108, 158. *see also* reclaiming witchcraft
  accusations, 5–6
  in Australian context, 28–30
  black, 138
  conjuring up new methods, 11–15
  contemporary, 7, 10, 12, 16, 45, 81, 101, 103
  Dianic, 27
  modern, 10
  power of, 138
  racial issue in, 29–30
  rejecting linearity of time, 116
  rituals in, 95–96, 103
  second wave feminism and, 10–11
  skill, 34
  studying in anthropology, 12
  war on witches, 97–100
  white, 42–43, 138
Witchcraft and Paganism in Australia (Hume), 12
The Witch Doesn't Burn in This One, (Lovelace), 162
Witches, Feminism and the Fall of the West (Dutton), 161
Witches, Sluts, Feminists (Sollee), 161
Witches, Witch-Hunting, and Women (Federici), 161
'Witch Hunt', 141, 147
witch reclamation, 154–155
  altars, 162–163
  covens, 159–161

  guidance and teachings of, 156
  hexes, 164–165
  resistance and refusal, 157–159
  use of resource books, 161–162
witchy/witch(es), 34, 134
  artwork, 163
  feminism, 7–11, 15–18, 148–149
  hunts, 2–3, 6
  witch-cult hypothesis, 99
  witch-hunting panic, 80
  women, power and, 4–7
'wokeism', 27
Wolfe, Patrick, 29
womanhood, 58
women, 100. *see also* Black women
  big three C's, 102
  biological essentialism, 103
  fear about, 125–127
  Lilith's story of oppression, 104–105
  matriarchal myth, 101
  oppression, successive cycles of, 101–102
  queer community archives, 105–106
  queer resistance, 104
  saving from sexual nature, 79–81
  sexist jokes on bodies, 143
  spirituality, 10, 58
  in Voodoo, 110, 112–113, 129
  witches, power and, 4–7
  women-only covens, 10
  women-only groups, 10, 59
Women's International Terrorist Conspiracy from Hell (W. I. T. C. H.), 135, 140
Words Are My Matter (Le Guin), 102

Zagarus (Olympian god), 35